SRA Imagine It!

Language Arts Handbook

Level 2

McGraw Hill SRA

Columbus, OH

Acknowledgments

Grateful acknowledgment is given to the following publishers and copyright owners for permissions granted to reprint selections from their publications. All possible care has been taken to trace ownership and secure permission for each selection included. In case of any errors or omissions, the Publisher will be pleased to make suitable acknowledgments in future editions.

A PICTURE BOOK OF MARTIN LUTHER KING, JR. Text copyright © 1989 by David A. Adler. Illustrations copyright © 1989 by Robert Casilla. All rights reserved. Reprinted by permission of Holiday House, Inc.

CESAR E. CHAVEZ by Don McLeese. Rourke Publishing LLC, Vero Beach, FL 32964.

IN THE MONEY © 2006 by Picture Window Books. All rights reserved.

From RED LIGHT, GREEN LIGHT, MAMA AND ME by Cari Best, Illustrated by Niki Daly. Published by Scholastic Inc./Orchard Books. Text copyright © 1995 by Cari Best, illustrations copyright © 1995 by Niki Daly. All rights reserved. Used by permission of Scholastic Inc.

AKIAK by Robert J. Blake. Copyright © 1997 by Robert J. Blake. Published by arrangement with Philomel Books, a division of Penguin Young Readers Group, a division of Penguin Group (USA) Inc. All rights reserved.

Text and art from THE EMPTY POT by Demi. © 1990 by Demi. Reprinted by permission of Henry Holt and Company, LLC.

From A LOG'S LIFE by Wendy Pfeffer, illustrated by Robin Brickman. Text copyright © 1997 by Wendy Pfeffer, Illustrations Copyright © 1997 by Robin Brickman. Reprinted by arrangement with Simon & Schuster Books For Young Readers, an Imprint of Simon & Schuster Children's Publishing Division. All rights reserved.

HOW THE GUINEA FOWL GOT HER SPOTS by Barbara Knutson. Copyright 1990 by Barbara Knutson. Used by permission of the estate. All rights reserved.

Photo Credits

9 © Micheal Newman/PhotoEdit; 55 © Steve Lyne/Dorling Kindersley/Getty; 81 © Alamy; 82 © tbkmedia.de/Alamy; 91 © Najlah Feanny/Corbis; 103 © David Frazier/PhotoEdit; 114 © Photodisc/Getty; 116 © Library of Congress; 123 © Micheal Newman/PhotoEdit; 137 © Dale C. Spartas/Corbis; 142 © Gary Rhijnsburger/Masterfile; 154 © Nordicphotos/Alamy; 158 © David Young-Wolff/PhotoEdit; 205 © Marin Schutt/dpa/Corbis; 208 © Keren Su/Corbis; 224 © Kevin R. Morris/Corbis; 238 © Richard Price/Getty; 251a © Johner Images/Getty; 251b © David Young-Wolff/PhotoEdit; 261 © Panoramic Images/Getty; 263 © Dietrich Rose/zefa/Corbis; 280 © BananaStock/Jupiter Images; 291 © Caroline Warren/Photodisc Red/Getty Royalty-Free; 298 © Millard H. Sharp/Photo Researchers, Inc; 308 © Bill Aron/PhotoEdit; 315 © Corbis; 321 © GK& Vikki Hart/Photonica/Getty; 328 © BananaStock/Alamy.

SRAonline.com

 SRA

Printed in the United States of America.

Send all inquiries to this address:
SRA/McGraw-Hill
4400 Easton Commons
Columbus, OH 43219-6188

ISBN: 978-0-07-622248-3
MHID: 0-07-622248-9

1 2 3 4 5 6 7 8 9 RRC 13 12 11 10 09 08

Table of Contents

You Are a Writer!

How do you describe yourself? You might tell how old you are. You may tell about your hobbies. You might talk about your favorite color or food. You could also say, "I'm a writer!"

You might think famous authors were born good writers. They worked hard to become good writers. No matter who you are, writing takes practice. The more you practice, the better your writing will be.

Why Should I Write?

Why should you write? Writing is a great way to share your feelings. Writing can also be fun. Here are some other reasons why people like to write.

"Writing helps me remember things."
                              —Kelly, age 8

"I love to share what I write with my class."
                              —Marcos, age 8

"Last week in the hall, I saw a sixth grader reading a poster I made!"
                              —Hani, age 8

How Can I Be a Writer?

Rosa never thought of herself as a writer. Then she began to think about the past week and made a list of all the kinds of writing she had done.

Take a Look

- my homework list
- my letter to Aunt Brenda
- my journal entry
- the birthday card I made for Dad
- the list of school supplies I need to buy
- a note to remember to get Jacob a present for his birthday party

Try It! Think of the things you have written this week at home and at school. Make a list like Rosa's.

What Is a Writer?

Anyone who writes is a writer. To be a writer, you need a reason, or purpose, to write.

There are many purposes for writing. You may write lists to help yourself remember things. You might write in a diary or journal. You may write a note or a letter to a friend. You are a writer in school when you take notes in class.

There is no secret to being a writer. There are many ways to become a better writer.

Using This Handbook

Everyone is a writer, but writing isn't always easy. Every writer needs help gathering ideas and beginning to write. Good writers follow a process that helps them write better. You can make your writing better if you follow a similar process.

Athletes and musicians need to practice to be the best at what they do. To be a better writer, you will need to practice.

Now are you starting to picture yourself as a writer?

The Pulitzer Prize, named after Joseph Pulitzer, is an award given to outstanding writers.

Traits of Good Writing

Good writing takes thought and practice. Writers aren't born as good writers. This lesson will introduce you to some traits of good writing. These are helpful tips to help you in the writing process.

Ideas

▶ All good writing is clear and easy to read. Good writing also says something interesting. Good writing has many details, and it has correct facts.

Organization

▶ Good writing begins with a good opening. Information should be in order. Think about what readers need and want to know. Good writing presents the main idea in an interesting way.

Voice

▶ The writer's voice is his or her way of saying things. It helps the readers get to know the writer. A writer's personality comes through in writing with *voice*.

Word Choice

▶ A writer paints a picture with words. Good word choices make the writing interesting to read and easy to picture. Use words that help the reader see, feel, and hear your ideas, such as *sizzling* and *bumpy*. Use interesting verbs, such as *chuckled* and *crawled*.

Sentence Fluency

▶ Sentences in a paragraph should always stay on the topic. This helps the reader understand the paragraph.

Conventions

▶ Writing that has mistakes will confuse readers. Check for correct spelling, grammar, punctuation, and capitalization.

Presentation

▶ You should be proud of your work! Always make a clean and neat copy before anyone reads it. Add pictures or a drawing to make it look better. If you have a computer, try adding graphics or clip art. The way you present your work is very important.

Examples of Good Writing

▶ **Ideas** "In the Money: A Book About Banking" by Nancy Loewen gives interesting facts about banks.

> The very first banks were in ancient Mesopotamia. People used grain as money. Temples and palaces offered people safe places to store it.

▶ **Organization** *A Log's Life* by Wendy Pfeffer has a logical order that tells how the storm caused the tree to fall.

> One stormy day a strong wind whips through the forest. The old oak bends with every gust. Rain pelts its branches. Wind tosses its leaves through the air. Lightning flashes and sizzles down its trunk. A thunderous crack startles the porcupine sleeping nearby. The tall oak begins to topple.

More Examples of Good Writing

▶ **Voice** Listen to the childlike voice in "Red Light, Green Light, Mama and Me" by Cari Best.

> I know Mama's desk as soon as I see the bumpy crocodile I made for her last year. I see puppets and puzzles and music and crayons.

▶ **Word Choice** "How the Guinea Fowl Got Her Spots," retold by Barbara Knutson, uses words that sound like the active noises they represent.

> She scratched and scrambled up the bank as fast as she could and whirred right between Cow and Lion, kicking and flapping in the dust.

▶ **Sentence Fluency** In "Akiak: A Tale From the Iditarod" by Robert J. Blake, the sentences vary between long and short to create a sense of rhythm.

> She did. Six hours after Mick and the team had left, Akiak padded softly, cautiously, into the checkpoint.

More Examples of Good Writing

▶ **Conventions** "The Empty Pot" by Demi shows good examples of punctuation, capitalization, and spelling.

> The next day a proclamation was issued: All the children in the land were to come to the palace. There they would be given special flower seeds by the Emperor. "Whoever can show me their best in a year's time," he said, "will succeed me to the throne."

▶ **Presentation** Jeff added photos to his poster on dinosaurs to make it more interesting to read.

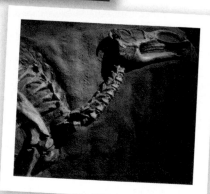

I like reading about dinosaurs.

Reading Your Writing

Using all of these traits will make your work clear and interesting. Your readers will understand and enjoy what you write.

Tips for Good Writing

Ideas

▶ Are your ideas interesting?

Organization

▶ Do you have an interesting opening?

▶ Are the events in the right order?

▶ Does your ending give readers things to consider?

Voice

▶ Did you say things in your own way?

Word Choice

▶ Did you paint a picture with your words?

Sentence Fluency

▶ Do your sentences stay on the topic?

Conventions

▶ Did you use capital letters for proper nouns, *I*, and at the beginning of each sentence?

▶ Have you checked for correct spellings?

▶ Did you use the right end mark after each sentence?

Presentation

▶ Did you make a clean and neat copy?

▶ Can you add pictures or clip art?

▶ Will your work look appealing to your readers?

The Writing Process

Learning to write can be fun. The writing process can help. There are five parts to the writing process: prewriting, drafting, revising, editing/proofreading, and publishing. You can use them to become a better writer.

The Writing Process

The writing process is a plan that anyone can follow. Each step will help you write clearly.

Prewriting

Prewriting is what you do before you start to write. Think about the kind of writing you are going to do. Decide on your topic. Make notes about what you want to say. Plan your writing.

Drafting

During this step, you write. Don't worry about making mistakes. Just get your ideas down on paper. Use your prewriting notes to help you.

1. Prewriting

2. Drafting

Revising

Reread your work. Will it make sense to readers? Can you add any details to make it clearer? Do you need to take out anything that doesn't belong? Should you put things in a different order?

Editing/Proofreading

Check your paper carefully and correct any mistakes in punctuation, capitalization, and spelling. Ask a classmate to help you look for mistakes in your work.

Publishing

The final step is to write or type on a computer a neat copy of your work. Then you can decide how to share it with others.

Prewriting: Getting Started

If you were taking a long trip, you'd use a map and plan your trip before you leave. Writers plan their writing like travelers plan their trips.

Prewriting is an important part of the writing process. It is a plan for your writing.

What Kind of Writing?

What kind of writing do you need or want to do?

There are many kinds of writing you can do. Here are just a few:

▶ poems
▶ stories
▶ reports
▶ songs
▶ plays
▶ letters
▶ lists

Who Is Your Audience?

Your readers are your audience. Are you writing for other students in your class? Is it just for you? Is it for one special person? Once you know whom you are writing to, think about what your audience needs or wants to know.

What Is Your Purpose?

You need to think about your reason, or purpose, for writing. Are you writing to entertain your audience? Maybe you want to give your audience information about something. Perhaps your goal as a writer is to change someone's mind.

Looking for Ideas

There are many places to get ideas about what to write. Some writers keep a notebook. Just write down ideas whenever you get them.

Here are some ideas.

- ▶ things people say and do
- ▶ things you think about
- ▶ things you hear about in the news
- ▶ books you read
- ▶ things you can teach others
- ▶ things you learn in school
- ▶ things you do with your friends

Ruben loved reading the book *Charlotte's Web* by E. B. White. The book gave him a great writing idea. He is going to write about his pet hamster, Sam.

Choosing a Topic

Choose a topic that you know a lot about or that interests you. Think about your audience. What topic might be interesting or important to them?

Gathering Facts

Once you decide on your topic, you might need to learn more about it. The library is a good place to go for facts on a topic. You can use atlases and encyclopedias. You can also use the Internet to find some information. Talk to other people who know a lot about the topic. Make sure you gather facts about your topic. Stay focused on your topic, or your audience will get confused.

Ruben wants to learn more about hamsters. He borrowed two books from the library. He also looked up information on the Internet at school.

Planning Your Writing

The next step is to make notes about what you want to write. There are many ways to put your ideas together.

▶ list facts
▶ draw pictures
▶ make webs
▶ find out meanings of words you don't know

These notes are for you to use as you write.

Take a Look

Ruben decided to use a web to plan his writing.

Did Ruben's web have interesting information on hamsters? Did his notes stay on the topic? Do you think he has enough ideas for his writing?

What are some topics or ideas you could use for writing? Choose something that interests you.

Reading Your Writing

Prewriting takes time, but it is one of the most important steps in writing. Without a plan your writing might not make sense to your audience. Also, your writing might be missing important ideas.

FUN FACT

A golden hamster can live as long as ten years.

Drafting: Beginning to Write

Now that you have planned your writing, it's time to write. Turn your notes into sentences. Write as much as you can. Use your notes, but if you think of something new, write it down. Don't worry about making mistakes. You can fix mistakes later.

Tips for Writing

▶ Write on one side of the paper, so you can cut it apart if you need to revise later.

▶ Leave space so you can add more later.

▶ Leave blanks when you don't know something.

▶ If you don't know how to spell a word, write the first letter and then as many other letters as you can.

Ruben used his web to plan a report about hamsters. It's not the way he wants it yet, but he has his ideas on paper.

Hamsters

They are soft and furry. They have short tails. Hamsters are easy to train and they make good pets. What do hamsters eat? They eat fruits, grain and vegetables. Hamsters carry their food in pouches. Everyone should get a hamster!

Reading Your Writing

Beginning to write will be easier if you remember to use your prewriting notes. Your notes or webs will help you put your ideas on paper. If you think of something new, always write that down, too.

Revising

You can make your writing better by changing parts of it. Making changes to improve your writing is called **revising.** Good writers use these tips when revising their work.

Tips for Good Writing

Ideas

▶ Is the main idea clear?

▶ Should any details be added?

▶ Is there any detail that isn't about the topic?

Organization

▶ Does my work have a beginning, a middle, and an end?

Sentence Fluency

▶ Do my sentences stay on the topic?

Word Choice

▶ Did I choose the best words to express my ideas?

Voice

▶ Will my audience want to keep reading?

Finally, compare your paper with your prewriting notes. Did you forget anything?

Ways to Fix Your Writing

Now make changes to your writing to be sure it says what you want it to say. Use these tips to revise your writing.

> ▶ Use arrows to move words and sentences.
>
> ▶ Use numbers to change the order of ideas.
>
> ▶ Cross out words or sentences that don't belong.
>
> ▶ Use scissors to cut apart the writing and use paste or tape to change the order of sentences or paragraphs.
>
> ▶ Use a caret (^) to put in new details or words.

Don't worry about misspellings or neatness when you revise. Focus on your ideas and how you express them.

Making Your Writing Clear

When you revise your writing, you need to make sure it is clearly written and makes sense. Be sure your ideas are written in the right order. To make your writing clear, ask yourself these questions.

Does my writing have

▶ an interesting beginning that tells the topic or main idea?

▶ a middle that gives important details about the topic or main idea?

▶ an ending that closes the writing in an interesting way?

▶ transition words such as *first, then, next,* and *finally,* that help the reader know which parts are the beginning, middle, and end?

After you answer these questions, you can make changes so your writing is easier to understand.

Take a Look

Below is Taylor's revision of a paragraph he wrote. See how he has marked his writing to put his ideas in order.

There are lots of ways to make people smile. Smile at your classmates. In the morning, help fix breakfast. Leave your room neat. Put your toys away. Let a friend sit by the window on the bus. Say thank you when your teacher helps you with a math problem. These things will make people smile!

Try It! Reread Taylor's work. How many places can you find where he can add words to make the order of the ideas clear?

Holding a Conference

A writer's conference is when you share your work with a teacher or classmates. They can help make your writing better.

What a Conference Looks Like

Every conference needs a writer and at least one listener. Sometimes there is a small group of three or four listeners.

Important Conference Rules

Every conference needs to follow important rules to make it helpful to the writer.

▶ Be polite.
▶ Listen carefully.
▶ Talk quietly and take turns speaking.
▶ Stay on the topic.

What the Writer Does

The writer has some important jobs to do to make the conference helpful.

1. Read the writing aloud. Practice reading before the conference.
2. Answer questions from the listeners.
3. Write down what the listeners say.

What the Listeners Do

The listeners also have important jobs to do to make the conference a success.

1. Listen quietly and carefully.
2. Show respect for the writer and the writing.
3. Ask questions about things you don't understand.
4. Tell what you like about the writing.
5. Make helpful suggestions that may make the writing better.

Taylor asked Terrell and Cindy to help him with his writing. He read to them. Here are their comments.

Terrell: I like that you told real things a person can do to help other people.

Cindy: You gave some good ideas for things to do at school.

Terrell: You could change your first sentence to a question to get people's attention.

Cindy: Maybe you could add more ways people can help their parents.

After the Conference

Taylor wrote what Cindy and Terrell said. Then he thanked them for their help. Next he will take their comments and decide what he is going to change. He will make changes to improve his writing.

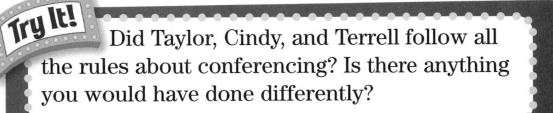

Try It! Did Taylor, Cindy, and Terrell follow all the rules about conferencing? Is there anything you would have done differently?

Reading Your Writing

Conferencing helps improve your writing. It helps you make sure that you are telling your audience what they need to know. It also helps you check that your work makes sense.

Editing/Proofreading

You have revised your writing so your ideas are clear and in the right order. Now it's time to read your writing to look for mistakes.

Here are some things to check.

▶ spelling
▶ punctuation
▶ capitalization

You can use a colored pencil, marker, or pen to mark these mistakes. You also will need a dictionary to help you with spelling.

Proofreading

Here are some proofreading marks to use to correct your work.

¶	Begin a paragraph.
∧	Add something.
ℒ	Take out something.
≡	Make a capital letter.
/	Make a small letter.
sp	Check spelling.
⊙	Add a period.

Using Proofreading Marks

Use these marks in a different color to fix your paper quickly. Look carefully at the examples for each mark.

¶ **Begin a paragraph.**
  ¶It is the easiest sandwich to make. First you get the cheese, the bread, and the butter together.

∧ **Add words.**
  Had the house been there for ∧ years? (many)

℘ **Take out, or delete, words or punctuation.**
  The dog dog ran away.

≡ **Change to a capital letter.**
  washington, D.C., is the nation's capital.

/ **Change to a small letter.**
  Harley hid behind the old Tree.

sp **Check spelling; write the correct spelling above the word.**
  Tad wore a green cotten sweater. (sp cotton)

⊙ **Add a period.**
  The dog ran quickly across the road⊙

Using an Editing/Proofreading Checklist

Before you write or type a final, neat copy, use the checklist below. This will help you find mistakes. You can also ask a classmate to help you check. Don't forget to make your proofreading marks in a different color. Have a dictionary handy for you to use too.

▶ Does each sentence begin with a capital letter?

▶ Does each sentence end with the correct punctuation?

▶ Are any words missing, or are there any words that don't belong?

▶ Are words spelled correctly?

▶ Is each paragraph indented?

After you have checked your paper, you are ready to copy or type your paper neatly.

Using a Computer to Edit/Proofread

Most computers can check your spelling, but be careful. The underlined word in the sentence below is not correct. The correct word is *their*. *There* is a real word, so a computer would not catch that mistake.

The children put <u>there</u> coats on the bed.

FunFact

Computers are not just in a computer lab. There are computers in cars, mp3 players, cellular phones, and grocery store scanners.

Reading Your Writing

If you don't edit/proofread your work, mistakes keep the reader from understanding your ideas. You can use a checklist to help you correct your work.

Publishing Your Writing

Once you write or type a neat copy of your work, you may decide to share it with others. This sharing is called **publishing.**

Ways to Publish Your Writing

▶ Display it on a bulletin board.

▶ Put it in a class book.

▶ Read it aloud to the class.

▶ Perform it in front of an audience.

▶ Send it to a magazine or newspaper.

▶ Put the writing to music.

▶ Perform your writing for your class.

▶ Put on a puppet show or a play.

▶ Print a nice copy on the computer at school.

Sometimes you can work with other classmates to publish. Each student can do a different job to get ready for sharing. Be creative!

Getting Your Writing Ready to Publish

After you have fixed the mistakes, you can neatly handwrite or type your work. Before you do that, you need to think about how you want your finished work to look. This is called **presentation.**

Ideas for Presenting Your Writing

▶ kinds and colors of paper

▶ kinds and colors of pens or ink

▶ extra materials you might need for publishing, such as staples, yarn, and cloth for book covers

▶ drawings or photos

▶ charts, graphs, or tables

If you can use a computer, here are some ideas for publishing your writing.

▶ change the font color

▶ add graphics or clip art

Keeping a Writing Portfolio

A **portfolio** is a place to keep your writing. You can include many different types of writing in your portfolio. In one part of your portfolio, you can keep your finished work.

A portfolio may contain

- ▶ stories
- ▶ poems
- ▶ letters
- ▶ reports
- ▶ comic strips
- ▶ plays
- ▶ reading journals
- ▶ songs

Keeping a portfolio is a good way for you, your teacher, and your family to see what you have learned as a writer. It is also fun to look back over work you have written.

Other Parts of Your Portfolio

You can label the different parts of your portfolio.

Writing Ideas

Good writers always keep ideas. Ideas can come from things that happen to you, books you read, talks with your friends, or things you learn in school. Not every idea will be used for writing.

Unfinished Writings

You may decide not to finish a writing. Don't throw it away. It doesn't matter whether it's prewriting notes or a revision. Keep it in your portfolio.

Special Words

Use one section of your portfolio to list special words. List words from units you study. Keep a list of words you learn and want to use. List words that you have trouble spelling.

FUN FACT

The word *publish* comes from a French word meaning "to make public."

Reading Your Writing

Your portfolio is a place that will show you and others how you've grown as a writer.

Following the Writing Process

Everyone in Maylee's second-grade class has to write a paragraph about something that happened to them over the summer.

Prewriting

First Maylee looked through the idea section of her writing portfolio for an idea. She found a good idea. She decided to tell about when her family got ready for a big storm.

Next Maylee thought about her audience. What would they need to know?

Then Maylee made notes to help her plan her paragraph. She put her notes in the order that things happened.

Take a Look

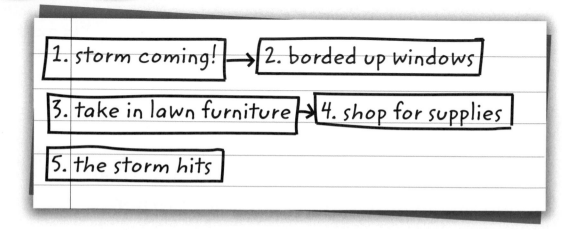

1. storm coming! → 2. borded up windows

3. take in lawn furniture → 4. shop for supplies

5. the storm hits

Writing a Draft

When Maylee finished planning her writing, she was ready to write. She used her notes as she wrote quickly. Maylee remembered not to worry about mistakes. She just worked on getting her ideas down.

Take a Look

A hurricane was coming in the ocean. Ocean water is salty. We had to hurry and get ready. We went to the store and got supplies. Dad put bords on all the windows. The windows had glass in them. The storm was over! I was glad we were ok.

Conferencing

Maylee's teacher asked Riley and Sara to listen as Maylee read to them. They listened quietly. Then Maylee wrote down what they said.

Riley: I like what you're writing. Hurricanes are exciting.

Sara: It was good you put important things to do to get ready for the storm.

Riley: I think you need an interesting or exciting first sentence to start your paragraph.

Sara: I think you have sentences that don't belong. You might take those out of your paragraph.

Riley: Your paragraph would be better if you added more details, like—what did you buy at the store?

Maylee thanked her two classmates. She thought they had good ideas about making her paragraph better.

Revising

Maylee reread her work carefully. Then she used some of the ideas from the conference to improve her work. She needed to make sure it was clear.

Take a Look

The Longest Nite

One day a hurricane was in the ocean not far from us. First my mom and I put the lawn furniture in the garadge. dad borded up the windows then we went to the store to by water candles bateries and flashlites. The wind was blowing so hard the trees bent over the ground. by morning the storm was over. I was glad no one in my family got hurt.

Try It!

Did Maylee make all the changes? Is there anything else you think she should change?

Editing/Proofreading

Maylee reread her work again. Now it has everything she wanted it to have. Next she needs to fix any mistakes in her writing. She will use a different color pencil and proofreading marks to mark the mistakes. She will do a final check using her editing checklist.

Take a Look

The Longest ~~Nite~~ Night

One day, a hurricane was in the ocean not far from us. First my mom and I put the lawn furniture in the ~~garadge.~~ garage. dad ~~borded~~ boarded up the windows. then we went to the store to ~~by~~ buy water, candles, ~~bateries~~ batteries, and ~~flashlites.~~ flashlights. The wind was blowing so hard the trees bent over the ground.! by morning the storm was over. I was glad no one in my family got hurt.

Publishing

Maylee wrote her paragraph neatly after she corrected the mistakes. She decided to draw pictures to show the important things that happened in her paragraph. Then she read her paragraph to the class. The pictures made it easy to see everything Maylee and her family did to get ready for the storm.

Take a Look

Here are the pictures that Maylee drew for her presentation.

Reading Your Writing

When you follow all of these steps, your writing will be interesting and will make sense to your readers.

FUN FACT

For a storm to be called a hurricane, its winds have to be over 72 miles per hour.

Forms of Writing

This is the part of the Handbook where you can find out how to write letters, reports, stories, descriptions, poetry, and much more. All the different kinds of writing you do are included here, plus some other kinds you may not have tried yet. Are you ready? Then let's get started.

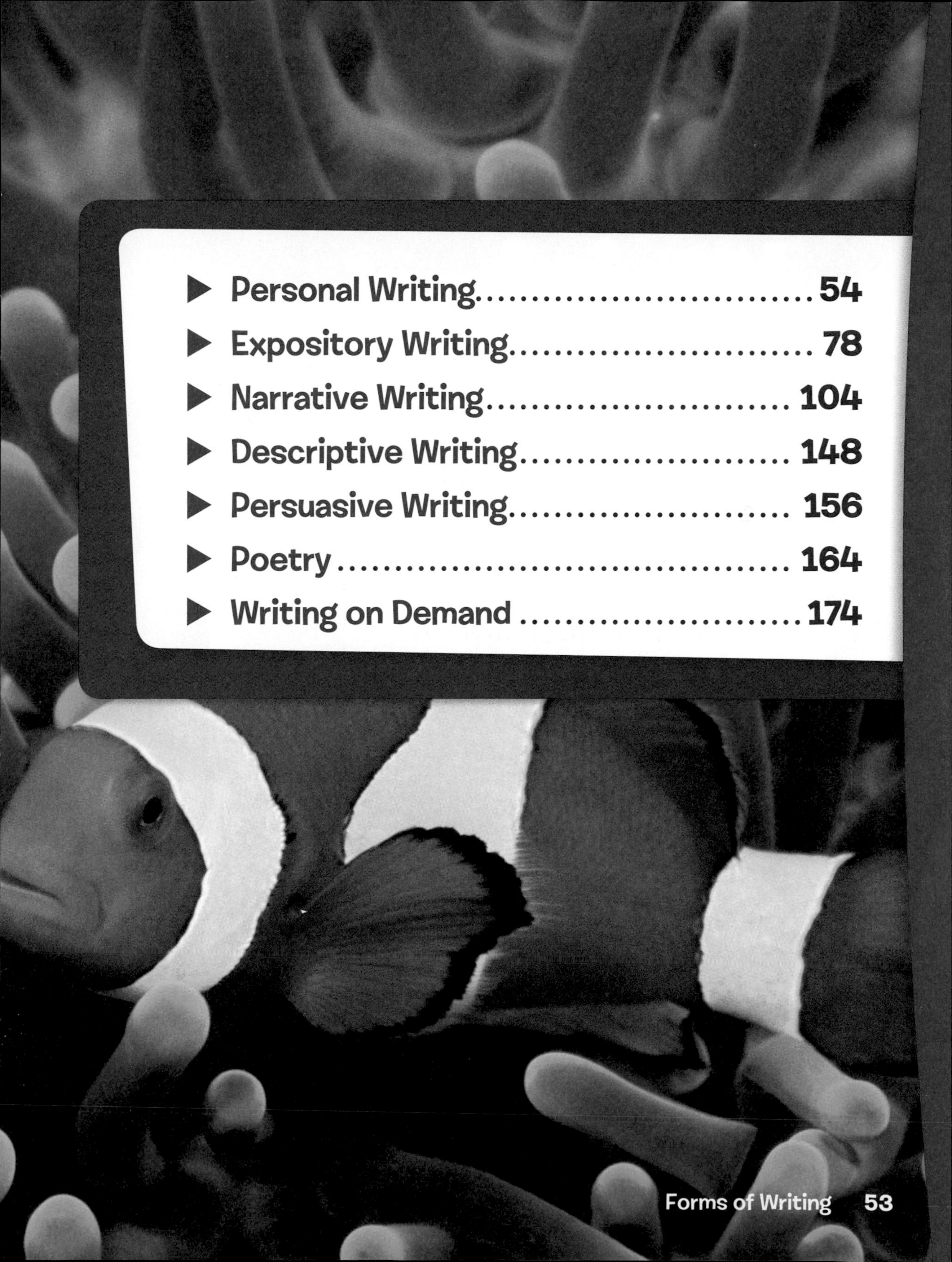

Forms of Writing

Personal Writing

Do you make lists to remind yourself to do things?

Do you write notes to your friends?

These are examples of personal writing. Look on the next page for more kinds of personal writing you can do.

Lists

Lists help us remember things. Lists are clear and easy to read. When you write lists, use words or short phrases. You don't need to use sentences. Here are some different kinds of lists.

To-Do Lists

A list can help you remember to do different things. Number your list if there is an order to follow.

Take a Look

Rita is pet sitting for her neighbor. She lists the jobs she needs to do every day so she doesn't forget anything.

1. feed fish, dog, cat, and bird
2. take dog for a walk
3. brush dog and cat
4. give bird, cat, and dog water
5. clean birdcage

Lists of Items

You can write lists of things you need to make a recipe, do a project, or buy at the store.

Mikala is going to make a treat to take to class for her birthday. She takes a shopping list to the store. It helps her get everything she needs.

- apples
- peanut butter
- chopped nuts
- napkins

Think about a list you made lately. What kind of list was it? Who was the audience for your list?

Reading Your Writing

When you make a list, write only the words you need to remember. Don't write sentences.

Journals

A **journal** is a place of your own where you can write about all of the things that matter to you. Every day you think and do many things that you can write about in your journal.

Write in your journal every day. Write about what you see, hear, or think. It's fun to reread your journal later. It helps you remember important things. A journal is also a good place to find ideas for writing.

What to Write in Your Journal

There are no rules about what to put in your journal. Here are a few ideas.

- things you hear and see
- what you think
- what happens to you
- poems
- songs
- photos or drawings
- funny or interesting sayings
- jokes or funny stories
- lists of ideas for writing topics
- lists of words you like

Things to Remember

1. Write in your journal every day.

2. Write the date.

3. Don't worry about mistakes.

4. Write about different things.

5. Be creative.

6. It's your own writing place.

Take a Look

Here is a page from Neil's journal.

October 7--I brought my pet gerbil 'Roo to school today. The class liked to watch him eat. Taylee made a loud noise. 'Roo jumped out of the cage. We found him in the boys' bathroom. It took 10 of us to find him.

November 12--Don't forget to make my costume for the play. I'll need
- poster paper
- orange paint
- old t-shirt
- old pants

Personal Thoughts

Adding **personal thoughts** to a personal narrative will tell readers about your thoughts and feelings. Using personal thoughts will hold a reader's attention and make your story more interesting.

Take a Look

Max wants to write about his trip to the circus. He writes a list of details in order. Then he adds a personal thought to each event.

1. tickets as a birthday present
   I had asked for circus tickets. I was pretty sure they were in the box.
2. family drove to the big top
   Everyone was crowded in the car. I didn't mind because I was so excited about the circus. We were singing songs on the way.
3. watched the performers and animals
   I couldn't take my eyes off the acrobats. My favorite thing was watching the elephants.
4. ate popcorn
   It tasted great.
5. went home
   The circus was as wonderful as I thought it would be. I'd love to go again.

Student Model

Here is the narrative Max wrote.

I have always wanted to go to the circus. I asked Mom and Dad for tickets for my birthday. When I opened my last present, I was pretty sure it was the tickets.

I was right! My family was going to the circus! Mom, Dad, my sister, and my grandparents crowded into our car. I didn't mind because I was so excited. We sang songs on the way. When we got to the big top, we watched different acts. It was all so exciting! The acrobats were amazing. I couldn't take my eyes off them. It was fun to watch all the animals. I think the elephants were my favorite. Another fun part of the circus is the food. The popcorn tasted great. The circus was as wonderful as I thought it would be. I would like to go back for my next birthday!

Try It!

Think of an important event in your life. What are some of your personal thoughts and feelings about this event?

Learning Logs

A **learning log** is a kind of journal where you can keep a record of what you learn. You might keep a learning log about a science or a history project. You may want to keep a different log for each subject. You can also keep a learning log for many subjects.

Your learning log might have some or all of these things:

- ▶ notes
- ▶ questions
- ▶ charts
- ▶ pictures or drawings with labels
- ▶ your thoughts or ideas

Try It!   Can you think of a subject you are studying now for which you might make a learning log? What kinds of information could you include?

Rachel's class is studying butterflies for an Earth Day project. In this project, they are raising butterflies from eggs. The students will let the butterflies go after they can fly.

Rachel made a learning log to chart the changes. She filled in the chart as she watched her butterfly grow.

Date	Stage	What it looks like
March 3	Egg	Size of pin
March 13	Larva	Small of my finger tip
April 1	Larva	2 inches long black and yellow
April 12	Chrysalis	On a branch Hanging by thread In a green case
April 20	Butterfly	Breaks out Wings are soft and wrinkled Flew away

Notes and Cards

It's fun to write notes to friends or family. Sometimes you just want to tell about something that happened to you. Sometimes you might have a special reason for sending a note. When you send a note, make sure the reason for the note is clear and that your note is easy to read. Always remember to sign your name.

Cards

You may want to write your note on paper. Other times you might want to write your message in a card. You can make a drawing or put a picture on the front. People like to get cards. It makes them feel good.

Thank-You Notes

It's a nice thing to send a thank-you note or card when someone gives you a gift. You also can send a thank-you note if someone does something nice for you. Make sure you say why you are thanking the person.

Take a Look

Here's a thank-you note Tony wrote.

Dear Aunt Winnie,

    Thank you for the great camera.
I like taking pictures. I've taken 24 already.
I will send some to you when I get them.

             Love,
             Tony

Get-Well Notes

Being sick is no fun. It makes you feel better when you get a card from someone. It helps to cheer you up. When you send cards to people who are sick, tell them you miss them. If you can, think of something funny to say or to draw to make them laugh.

Take a Look

Stevie misses his mom. Here is the get-well note he wrote to her.

Dear Mom,

    I am sorry you are sick. I can't wait until you come home.

                    Love,

                    Stevie

Invitations

If you have a party, you will want to send an invitation.

Invitations tell

▶ who is giving the party

▶ the reason for the party

▶ the time of the party

▶ the date of the party

▶ where the party is taking place

Take a Look

Matt sent out this invitation.

Dear Mindy,   ◀ Greeting

I am having a birthday party   ◀ Reason
on Friday, March 2, at 6:00 p.m.   ◀ When
The party is at my house. I live at
22 Willow Lane. Let me know if   ◀ Where
you can come. I hope you can!

                              Matt   ◀ Name

Friendly Letters

If you want to talk with friends or family who live nearby, you might walk to their house or call them on the telephone. When was the last time you talked to someone in another town or state?

What Is a Friendly Letter?

A **friendly letter** is a letter to a friend or relative. People like getting letters in the mail. A letter lets you think about what you really want to say. You can reread it and be sure it's just right.

E-mail is another type of a friendly letter. E-mail is just like writing a friendly letter, but your friend will get it faster. If you know someone with an e-mail address, try sending him or her a friendly e-mail.

Look at Sam's letter below. A friendly letter has five parts.

123 Rye Avenue
Millville, MN 73473
June 6, 2003

◀ **Heading**

Dear Aunt Grace,

◀ **Greeting**

Guess what I got? Last week I found a puppy hiding in the park. He was all muddy. He was scared and hungry. I took him home. Dad and I fed him and gave him a bath. We named him Patches. Write back soon.

◀ **Body**

Love,
Sam

◀ **Closing**
◀ **Signature**

Getting Your Friendly Letter Ready to Mail

When you're done writing your letter, fold it into three parts so it fits into an envelope.

Addressing Your Envelope

► Write your name, street address, city, state, and zip code in the top left corner.

► Write the name and street address of the person you're sending the letter to in the middle.

► Use post office abbreviations for state names.

► Don't forget to put a stamp in the upper right corner.

Take a Look

Here's what Sam's envelope looks like.

Sam Burns
123 Rye Avenue
Millville, MN 73473

◄ **Your name and address**

Stamp ▲

Mailing address ►

Grace Martin
203 Bay Street
Southport, NC 28477

Tips for Writing a Friendly Letter

Prewriting Make a Plan

▶ Who will get your letter?

▶ What does that person want to know?

▶ Ask about the person's life.

▶ Tell about your friends and family.

Drafting Put Your Thoughts on Paper

▶ Use your notes to write a letter.

▶ Don't worry about mistakes. You can fix those later.

Revising Be Sure It Makes Sense

▶ **Ideas** Did you include everything you want to say?

▶ **Organization** Did you stay on the topic?

Editing/Proofreading Look Closely at Details

▶ **Conventions** Does your letter have all five parts? Are people's names capitalized? Are the greeting and closing followed by commas?

Publishing Sending Your Friendly Letter

▶ **Presentation** Write or type a neat copy of your letter. Get your envelope ready and mail your letter.

Business Letters

You write a **business letter** when you need something or if you have a problem. When you write a business letter, you are writing to a company or to a person you don't know.

When to Write a Business Letter

Here are some reasons to write a business letter:

▶ to order or ask for something

▶ to complain about a problem

▶ to ask for information about something

▶ to share your opinions or ideas about something

Try It!

Is there something you would like to order? Is there something you would like to know? If there is, you can write a business letter.

What to Say in Your Business Letter

What you say in your letter depends on your reason for writing. Keep in mind the person who will get your letter. He or she will be more willing to help if your letter is clear and polite.

Writing to Ask for Something

► Tell who you are.

► Tell exactly what you want.

► Tell why you want it.

► Thank the person for helping you.

Writing to Complain about Something

► Tell who you are.

► Tell exactly what the problem is.

► Tell how you feel about the problem.

► Tell what should be done to fix the problem.

► Thank the person for reading your letter.

Reading Your Writing

Make sure your letter is clearly written. The person reading your letter may be more likely to answer.

Parts of a Business Letter

A business letter has six parts.

Heading

▶ The heading is the sender's name and address plus the date.

Inside Address

▶ The inside address is the name and address of the person getting your letter.

Salutation or Greeting

▶ The salutation greets whom you are writing. A colon should follow the name.
Dear Dr. Kirtley: Dear Ms. Adams:

▶ If you don't know the person's name, just write *Sir*, *Madam*, or the name of the company.

Body

▶ The body of the letter is where you tell about your problem or tell what you want to order.

Closing

▶ To end your letter, use one of these closings. Remember to use a comma.
Yours truly,   Sincerely,   Thank you,

Signature

▶ Write your first and last name.

Read Kipper's letter asking a zoo owner for information about polar bears.

Heading ▶
204 Laurel Drive
Oakmont, IL 50763
January 22, 2003

Inside
Address ▶
Ms. Arnold
Wildwood Zoo
27 Highland Park Drive
Fairmont, IL 50721

Salutation ▶
Dear Ms. Arnold:

Body ▶
My name is Kipper Murphy. I am in second grade at Hills Elementary School. Our class will be studying animals of the Arctic. I am doing a report on polar bears. I know you have some polar bears in your zoo. You must know a lot about them.

Could you send me any information you have about polar bears? I want to learn as much as I can for my report.

Closing ▶
Thank you,

Signature ▶
Kipper Murphy

Sending Your Business Letter

When your letter is neatly typed or written, you are ready to send it.

Addressing Your Envelope

Neatly address your envelope by writing your name and address in the upper left corner of the envelope. Write the name and address of the person in the lower center of the envelope.

Tips for Addressing Your Envelope

▶ Capitalize all names of people, companies, streets, cities, and states.

▶ Use the post office abbreviations for state names.

▶ Use a comma between the city and state.

▶ Don't forget to put a stamp in the top right corner of the envelope.

Kipper Murphy
204 Laurel Drive
Oakmont, IL 50763

Ms. Arnold
Wildwood Zoo
27 Highland Park Drive
Fairmont, IL 50721

Folding Your Business Letter

Neatly fold your letter in three equal parts. Put your letter into the envelope. Seal the envelope and put a stamp on it. It's ready to drop in the mailbox!

Tips for Writing Business Letters

Prewriting Make a Plan

▶ Think about the reason for your letter. Make some notes.

▶ Who is going to get your letter?

Drafting Put Your Thoughts on Paper

▶ Use your notes to write the letter.

▶ Make sure you have all six parts of the letter.

Revising Be Sure It Makes Sense

▶ **Ideas** Did you describe your problem or what you need?

▶ **Voice** Is your letter polite?

▶ **Organization** Did you stay on the topic?

Editing/Proofreading Look Closely at the Details

▶ **Conventions** Capitalize names of people and places, the salutation, and the first word of the closing. Use a colon after the salutation. Use a comma after the closing.

Publishing Get Your Letter Ready to Mail

▶ **Presentation** Make sure your letter is neatly written or typed. Then put it in the envelope, stamp it, and seal it.

Forms of Writing

Expository Writing

Expository writing does two things. It explains how to do something, or it gives information about something.

Suppose you wrote a report about your favorite animal. Suppose you wrote directions explaining how to make your favorite sandwich. Both are examples of expository writing.

Writing a Summary

A **summary** paragraph tells the main idea and important points of a longer piece of writing.

Read the following paragraphs from "A Picture Book of Martin Luther King, Jr" by David Adler.

> Martin Luther King, Jr. was one of America's great leaders. He was a powerful speaker, and he spoke out against laws which kept black people out of many schools and jobs. He led protests and marches demanding fair laws for all people.
>
> In 1963 Dr. King led the biggest march of all—the March on Washington. More than two hundred thousand black and white people followed him. "I have a dream," he said in his speech. "I have a dream that my four children will one day live in a nation where they will not be judged by the color of their skin but by the content of their character."
>
> On April 4 in Memphis, Dr. King stood outside his motel room. Another man, James Earl Ray, was hiding nearby. He pointed a rifle at Dr. King. He fired the gun. An hour later Dr. King was dead.

Summary Tips

▶ Always tell the main idea of each paragraph.
▶ The main idea is sometimes found near the beginning of each paragraph.
▶ Use your own words when you write a summary.
▶ Do not copy sentences from the paragraphs that you are summarizing.

Take a Look

Tory read the paragraphs about Martin Luther King, Jr. Then she wrote a summary of what she read.

> Martin Luther King, Jr. was a great American leader. He led protests against hate, prejudice, and violence. He was shot by James Earl Ray in April, 1968.

Try It! Can you think of anything Tory could add to her summary?

Giving Directions on How to Do Something

Sometimes you need to write directions for others. You will need to write clear directions so others can understand you.

Getting Ready to Write Directions

Planning is the most important step for this kind of writing. Think about all of the steps to do something. You need to make sure each step is in the right order. Also, think about your reader. Decide what your reader will need to know.

Take a Look

Nathan's friend Ben is keeping his dog for a week. Nathan wants Ben to give his dog a bath.

Fill the tub.

↓

Put dog in tub.

↓

Wash and rinse the dog.

↓

Take dog out and dry it.

Take a Look

Nathan used his notes to write directions for Ben on how to give the dog a bath.

> ## How to Give a Dog a Bath
>
> Here's how to give a dog a bath. First fill a tub with water. Make sure the water isn't too hot or too cold. Next put the dog in the tub. Then wash and rinse the dog. Finally take the dog out and dry him with a towel.

Try It! Check Nathan's plan with his writing. Did he remember to put everything in? Did he add anything?

Reading Your Writing

To be sure your directions make sense, list everything that is needed before you start writing.

Giving Directions to a Place

Sometimes you may be asked to write directions on how to get to a certain place. Think about what your reader needs to know to get there.

Things to Remember

▶ Use location words such as *left* and *right*.

▶ Stick to what the reader needs to know. Adding information that is not important will only make it harder to follow your directions.

▶ Put your steps in the right order.

Take a Look

Lindy was asked to write directions to the playground for parents who are coming to the school's field day activities. Look at her prewriting web.

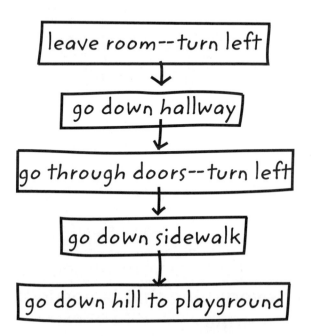

leave room--turn left

go down hallway

go through doors--turn left

go down sidewalk

go down hill to playground

Read Lindy's directions to the playground.

Getting to the Playground

1. Leave Mrs. Drake's classroom and turn left.
2. Go down the hallway past the library.
3. Go through the red double doors and turn left.
4. Walk down the sidewalk past the gym.
5. Go down the grassy hill to the playground.

Try It! Did Lindy follow her plan? What details did she add to make her writing more interesting and clear?

Reading Your Writing

Did you tell your reader everything they need to know? If you leave something out, someone may get lost.

Tips for Writing How to Do Something

Prewriting Make a Plan

▶ Picture the steps in your mind.

▶ Write your planning notes in order.

Drafting Put Your Thoughts on Paper

▶ Keep your notes in front of you so you don't forget any steps.

▶ As you write, you may think of other steps or things the reader might need.

Revising Be Sure It Makes Sense

▶ Did you forget any steps?

▶ Is each step in the right order?

▶ Did you use time and order words?

Editing/Proofreading Look Closely at the Details

▶ Did you check the spelling?

▶ Did you check the punctuation?

Publishing Share Your Work

▶ Neatly write or type your directions.

▶ Have someone try to follow your directions.

Tips for Writing Directions to a Place

Prewriting Make a Plan

▶ Think about where your reader needs to go.

▶ Start your directions from the place your reader is starting.

▶ Write your notes in the right order.

Drafting Put Your Thoughts on Paper

▶ Follow your notes carefully.

Revising Be Sure It Makes Sense

▶ **Ideas** Did you leave out any important details?

▶ **Organization** Are your steps in the right order?

▶ **Word Choice** Did you use place and location words?

Editing/Proofreading Look Closely at the Details

▶ **Conventions** Did you check the spelling?

Publishing Share Your Work

▶ **Presentation** Make a neatly written or typed copy.

▶ Draw a map for your reader.

Responding to Literature

Writing a response to literature helps you share your thoughts and feelings about a story. Analyzing a story can also help you better understand what you have read. A written response to literature can focus on the characters, the plot, or the setting of a story.

Character Analysis

Analyzing a character's thoughts, actions, and feelings will help you get to know the character. After reading a story, choose a character that interests you. Then ask yourself the following questions to help you plan your character analysis: *What is the character's role in the story? What does the character look like? How does the character feel? Which words does the author use to describe the character?*

Take a Look

After reading "Corduroy", Olivia decided to write a character analysis of Corduroy. She thought about the following questions to help her write her analysis: *What does Corduroy look like? How does he feel? Which words in the story are used to describe Corduroy?*

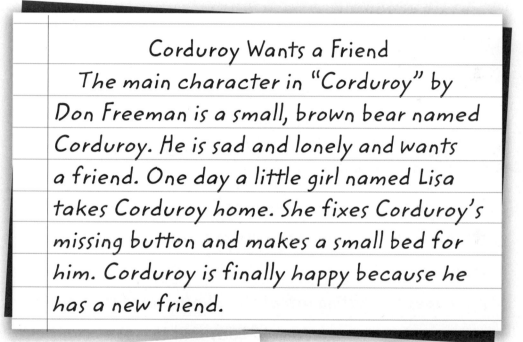

Corduroy Wants a Friend

The main character in "Corduroy" by Don Freeman is a small, brown bear named Corduroy. He is sad and lonely and wants a friend. One day a little girl named Lisa takes Corduroy home. She fixes Corduroy's missing button and makes a small bed for him. Corduroy is finally happy because he has a new friend.

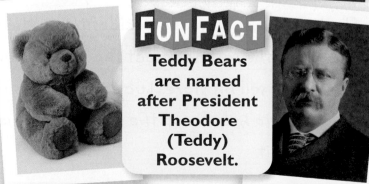

FUNFACT

Teddy Bears are named after President Theodore (Teddy) Roosevelt.

Setting Analysis

The setting is the time and place in which the events of a story take place. The setting affects the plot and helps develop the characters. Analyzing the setting of a story helps you better understand the characters and the plot. As you read, think about where and when the story takes place. Also, think about how the setting affects the story.

Take a Look

While reading *Grandpa's Corner Store*, Carlos takes notes about the setting.

1. When does the story take place? present day

2. Where does the story take place? grandpa's grocery store

3. How does the setting affect the characters? Grandpa's grocery store is important to Lucy and the community. She is sad when Grandpa decides to sell the store.

4. How does the setting affect the plot? Grandpa decides to sell his store. Lucy asks friends and neighbors to help fix up the store. Grandpa decides not to sell it.

Carlos used his notes to write a setting analysis for *Grandpa's Corner Store.*

> In *Grandpa's Corner Store* by DyAnne DiSalvo-Ryan, a new supermarket is opening in Lucy's town. Grandpa decides to sell his small grocery store. Lucy is sad. She feels that Grandpa's store is an important part of the community. Lucy asks friends and neighbors to help fix up the store. Everyone is glad to help. Grandpa realizes his store is an important part of the community.

Plot Analysis

The main events in a story make up the plot. An author arranges the events in a story carefully. All the events lead to the conclusion. A plot analysis can discuss the main problem in a story. An analysis can also describe how the main character solves the problem.

Take a Look

Megan plans to write a plot analysis of *The Hole in the Dike.* Look at her prewriting web.

Beginning ▶ Peter lives in Holland. He is riding his bicycle home from his friend's house. Along the way, he notices a small hole in the dike.

Middle ▶ Peter puts his finger in the hole to stop the leak. He tries to stop the leak with a stone and a stick. Nothing works. He cries for help, but no one hears him. He has to keep his finger in the hole all night. Then a milkman hears Peter shouting for help.

End ▶ The milkman tells the villagers about the hole. Many men come to help repair the leak. Peter is a hero because he saves Holland.

Tips for Writing a Response to Literature

Prewriting Make a Plan

▶ Read the story and take notes about the characters, the setting, and the plot.

▶ Use a web to organize your notes.

Drafting Put Your Thoughts on Paper

▶ Write your Response to Literature. Use your web as a guide.

▶ Include the title of the book and the name of the author.

Revising Revise

▶ **Ideas** Did you use details from the story to support your analysis?

▶ **Organization** Are all your ideas related to the topic?

Editing/Proofreading Look Closely at the Details

▶ Did you capitalize proper nouns and the beginnings of sentences?

▶ Did you italicize the title of the book?

▶ Did you check your spelling?

Publishing Share Your Response to Literature

▶ **Presentation** Neatly write or type your Response to Literature. Share your writing with your classmates.

▶ Draw an illustration for your writing.

Reports

When you write a report, you need to think about these questions.

▶ What is going to be your topic?

▶ How are you going to learn about it?

▶ How are you going to write about it?

If you take one step at a time, you and your readers will enjoy finding out about your topic.

Choosing a Topic

Think about topics that interest you. After you choose a topic, make sure it isn't too big. For example, the topic of animals is too big and covers too much information. You should choose one kind of animal, such as whales, for your report.

Finding Information

You can look in many places to get information about your topic.

▶ books

▶ magazines

▶ encyclopedias

▶ people who know about the topic

▶ Internet at school

Taking Notes

As you find out about your topic, you will need to take notes. You will use them later when you write your report. There are many ways to take notes.

▶ note cards

▶ charts

▶ webs

Here's how to use a web to organize your notes. Write your topic in the bubble in the middle of the web. Then write a question you have about your topic in each outside bubble. Ask yourself two or three questions. Then add your facts around each question bubble.

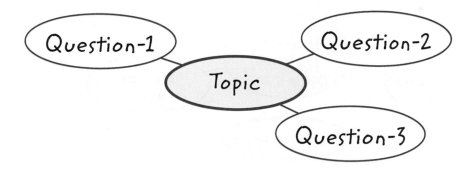

Take a Look

Katy used the web below to plan her report on whales. She chose what questions she wanted to answer. She used library books and magazines to find her answers. As she read about whales, she filled in the web with her notes.

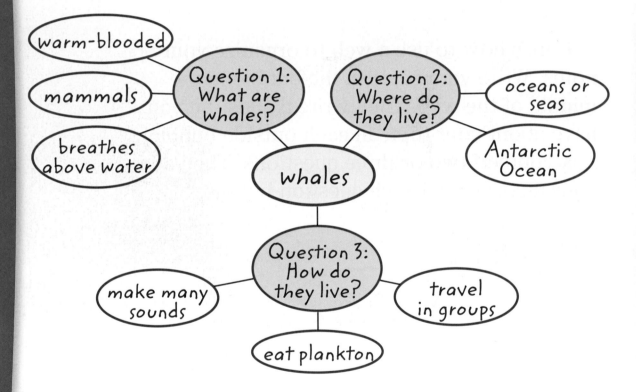

Katy used her notes to write her report on whales.

Whales

By Katy Floyd

What are whales? Whales are warm-blooded mammals. They need to come up to breathe the air above the water.

Where do whales live? They live in the water. They need water to hold their weight. Oceans and seas are the homes for whales. Many whales live in the Antarctic Ocean.

How do whales live? Many whales travel in groups. They make low sounds to talk to each other. They make high sounds to find food and to travel. They eat baby shrimp and plankton.

FUN FACT

The largest animal in the world is the blue whale, which can grow to over 100 feet long and weigh over 200 tons.

Tips for Writing a Report

Prewriting Make a Plan

▶ Choose the topic that interests you the most.

▶ Make sure your topic isn't too big.

▶ Ask yourself two questions about your topic.

▶ Use at least two sources to get your facts.

▶ Make notes using webs, charts, or note cards.

Drafting Put Your Thoughts on Paper

▶ Use your notes as you write your report.

Revising Be Sure It Makes Sense

▶ **Ideas** Did you put in all of your notes? Do you have any sentences or facts that don't belong?

▶ **Word Choice** Did you define hard words for your readers?

▶ **Organization** Are your facts in the right paragraphs?

Look Closely at the Details

▶ **Conventions** Check to be sure you have spelled any special words or names correctly.

▶ Make sure to indent each new paragraph.

▶ Don't forget to give your report a title.

▶ Capitalize any proper nouns and the main words in a title.

Publishing **Share Your Report**

▶ **Presentation** Neatly write or type a copy of your report.

▶ You may want to draw a picture or add photos to go with your report.

▶ You might share your report by reading it aloud to the class or to small groups of classmates.

News Story

A news story is a true report that informs readers about something interesting that happened recently. A news story should include facts rather than opinions.

News stories should include information that answers the following questions.

Who?	*Who* was involved, or *whom* does it affect?
What?	*What* did he or she do? OR *What* happened?
When?	*When* did the event take place?
Where?	*Where* did the event take place?
Why?	*Why* did the person do what he or she did? OR *Why* did the event happen?
How?	*How* did the event happen? OR *How* was the problem solved?

Writing a News Story

Headline is the title of a news story. It should grab the reader's attention. A **byline** tells who wrote the story.

Lead is the first paragraph in a news story.

Body is the remainder of the story.

Finding the Answers to the Questions

How do you find the answers to the questions? There are three ways:

1. **Observation:** If you saw or heard what happened, you can report based on that.

2. **Interviews:** If you did not see or hear what happened, you can talk to someone who was there.
   NOTE: Make sure the person you interview gives you only facts, not just what he or she thinks. A news story must be true and accurate so the reader can get the correct information.

3. **Research:** You can read books, articles, or search the Internet for more information about a news story.

Take a Look

Jane is a reporter for her elementary newspaper, and she just learned some information about school lunches for the next year. Her first step is to answer the questions. Her second step is to write a lead for the news story. Her last step is to fill in the details by interviewing students and teachers. Here is her full story.

School lunch prices to skyrocket after break

By Jane Walker

The school district will raise the price for a hot school lunch at the elementary school by fifty cents. The price will go from $2.50 to $3.00 after the winter break due to the cost of food.

Some people are upset that the price is going up. Some people understand and are not upset. Mr. Peters, a second-grade teacher, said, "Food prices are going up, so it makes sense that the cafeteria lunch price will go up too." He thinks that by spending a little more for our lunches, we can keep the quality good.

Maria, a third-grade student, said, "That will be $2.50 more every week. Some people do not have much money. I hope we will still be able to afford lunches." Other students feel the same way.

Mrs. Sanchez is the superintendent. She told me the school will help students pay for lunches if they cannot afford the new prices. That way the change will be okay for everybody.

Tips for Writing a News Story

Prewriting Make a Plan

Do you have the answers to the questions?

Drafting Put Your Thoughts on Paper

▶ Write a headline that lets your readers know the subject of the news story.

Revising Be Sure It Makes Sense

▶ **Ideas** Did you cover the questions in the lead?

▶ **Organization** Did you stick to the facts?

▶ **Voice** Did you convince your audience to read your news story?

▶ **Sentence Fluency** Did you tell your news story quickly and simply?

Editing/Proofreading Look Closely at the Details

▶ **Conventions** Check your spelling. If you are unsure of a word, look it up in the dictionary.

Publishing Share

▶ **Presentation** Make a clean copy of your news story so it is easy to read and appealing to your readers.

Forms of Writing

Narrative Writing

Narrative writing tells a story. The story can be true or make-believe. When you write a story, you are telling your readers what happened. Your story needs a beginning, a middle, and an end. It also needs a setting and characters. Look at the next page for some different kinds of stories you can write.

Personal Narratives

A **personal narrative** tells about something that has happened in your life.

Think of things that have happened to you. Those are all topics that you can write about in personal narratives.

Try It!

Which of these ideas could you use to write a personal narrative?

Tommy won a race.

A boy climbed a mountain.

I met a new friend.

Take a Look

Nick wants to write about teaching his dog tricks. First he uses a web to write his details in order.

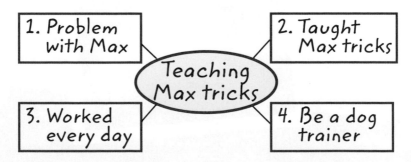

1. Problem with Max

2. Taught Max tricks

Teaching Max tricks

3. Worked every day

4. Be a dog trainer

Student Model

Here's the personal narrative that Nick wrote.

I had a problem with my puppy. Max was cute, but he didn't know how to do much. I wanted him to shake with his paw and fetch a stick. I worked with Max every day after school. I taught him to shake, fetch, and roll over! Max is now a smart dog. Maybe I will be a dog trainer when I get older.

Reading Your Writing

Your personal narrative should be about something that really happened in your life. Make sure you stick to your topic.

Tips for Writing a Personal Narrative

 **Prewriting**   Make a Plan

▶ Make a list of things that have happened to you lately.

▶ Pick one idea from your list for your topic.

▶ Make a web to organize your ideas.

 Drafting   Put Your Thoughts on Paper

▶ Write your personal narrative. Use your web.

▶ Don't worry about mistakes. You can correct them later.

Revising   Be Sure It Makes Sense

▶ **Ideas** Is it something that really happened to you?

▶ Is it something of interest to someone else?

▶ **Organization** Do you tell the events in order?

Look Closely at the Details

▶ **Conventions** Check the spelling.

▶ Make sure you capitalized proper nouns.

Publishing **Share Your Personal Narrative**

▶ **Presentation** Make a neatly typed or written final copy.

▶ Draw pictures to go with your personal narrative.

Autobiography

An **autobiography** is a story about a person's life written by that person. Facts and important events from the person's life are told in the order in which they happened.

When you write an autobiography, divide your life's events into three categories: past, present, and future.

Past

Begin with facts about when you were born.
▶ Your name
▶ When and where you were born
▶ Other members of your family (parents, brothers, sisters, and so on)

Present

Write about your life today.
▶ City and state where you live
▶ Whom you live with now
▶ Where you go to school
▶ Things you like and dislike
▶ Activities and friends

Future

Explain what you think your future will be like.

▶ What will your job be?

▶ Will you get married and have kids?

▶ Where will you live?

▶ What activities will you like to do?

Remember that an autobiography includes facts about a person's life. You need to write specific information about events that have happened to you. It is also important for you to write your ideas in the order in which they happened. The story must be written in the first-person point of view because it is a story about your life.

Try It!

Which of these ideas could you use to write your autobiography?

Vicki sang a solo at the concert.

The boy lost his dog.

I live in Columbus, Ohio.

Rebecca is writing an autobiography. First she uses a timeline to write down important events and dates from her life.

Born	Moved to Georgia	Sister was born	Began second grade
1999	2001	2004	2006

Next Rebecca makes notes on other important things about her life.

Past	Present	Future
born May 4, 1999 in Birmingham, Alabama	in second grade Jackson Elementary	be a ballerina
moved to Georgia for Dad's job	learning ballet	go to college
lived with parents	read books and ride my bike with friends	learn how to drive a car
younger sister Alice born in 2001		live in New York City

Student Model

Finally Rebecca used her timeline and notes to write her autobiography.

The Story of Rebecca

My name is Rebecca Ann Miller. I was born on May 4, 1999, in Birmingham, Alabama. I was my parents' first child. My mom's name is Tina Miller, and my dad's name is Randy Miller. My family moved to Atlanta, Georgia, in 2001 because my dad got a new job. When I was one and a half years old, my sister Alice was born on October 12, 2001.

In 2006, I started the second grade at Jackson Elementary. My teacher is Mr. Henderson. My best friend Laura is in my class. I take ballet classes once a week. This is my third year learning ballet, and it is my favorite thing to do! When I am not dancing, I like to read books in my room and ride bikes with my friends.

When I am older, I would like to go to college and be a ballerina. I plan to live in New York City. I think this is a good place to live if you want to be a professional dancer. I am looking forward to learning how to drive a car. I think it will be fun to be a grown up.

Biography

A **biography** is a real story about someone's life. Biographies can be written about anybody. It is important that a biography is written using only facts about the person. A biography also tells about the events in a person's life in the order in which they happened.

Biographies Might Include:

▶ The dates of a person's birth and death

▶ Information about the person's family

▶ Quotations from the person

Research

If the person is well-known or famous, you can find information in newspapers, magazines, encyclopedias, books, or on the Internet. Make sure you take lots of notes, and always write down the name of the source where you found your information.

Student Model

Here is the biography that Brett wrote.

Harriet Tubman was born in about 1820. Her name was Araminta Ross. She was sold into slavery. In 1834 she was hit in the head by her owner and was injured badly. She married John Tubman in 1844. Harriet learned about the Underground Railroa and ran away from her plantation in 1849.

From 1850 to 1860, Harriet Tubman rescued her family and over 300 other slaves. She helped free many slaves for over ten years. She saved hundreds of slaves. In 1863 she was a scout for the Civil War. That means she spied on people and watched out for Confederate soldiers.

In 1867 Harriet Tubman's husband died. Harriet Tubman married another man in 1869. His name was Nelson Davis. He died in 1888. When Harriet was about 83 years old, she gave her home and land to a church. They turned her land into a home for elderly people. Harriet Tubman died in 1913. She was a brave woman.

Tips for Writing a Biography

Prewriting   Make a Plan

▶ Interview your subject, or do research to learn more about him or her.

Drafting   Put Your Thoughts on Paper

▶ Write your thoughts down quickly.

Revising   Be Sure It Makes Sense

▶ **Organization** Are the events in the order in which they happened?

▶ **Word Choice** Did you choose descriptive words to write about the person?

Editing/Proofreading   Look Closely at the Details

▶ **Conventions** Did you use quotations correctly?

Publishing   Share

▶ **Presentation** Write a clean copy in the form of a book.

Realistic Stories

A **realistic story** is a story that did not happen, but the characters, places, and events in the story seem real.

Parts of a Realistic Story

▶ Characters do things that people or animals might do.

▶ Places in the story are real or seem real.

▶ Events in the story could really happen.

▶ A realistic problem is solved.

Try It!

Which of the ideas below could you use to write a realistic story?

▶ A flying frog saves the world.

▶ A boy wins a singing contest.

▶ A dog rides a bike.

Here's the realistic story that Gemma wrote.

The Party

    Juanita was worried. She was afraid that nobody would come to her party. She knew her friend Nikki would be there. What if no one else came? She would feel awful.

    Juanita looked out the window. She didn't see anyone. She couldn't watch anymore. She went into the kitchen to wait.

    Suddenly, the doorbell rang! She opened the door. There were kids on the porch. After a few minutes, more kids came.

    Later, Juanita's mom asked her if she had fun. She said she had a great time! She had worried for nothing.

Try It!

What are some ideas for a realistic story?

Reading Your Writing

Remember to make all the characters and events in your story seem real. If Juanita had a cartoon character at her party, it would not have been a realistic story.

Tips for Writing a Realistic Story

Prewriting   Make a Plan

▶ Make a list of ideas for your story. Choose the one you like the best.

▶ Choose a setting, a problem to be solved, and the characters for your story.

Drafting   Put Your Thoughts on Paper

▶ Write your realistic story. Use your notes.

▶ Don't worry about mistakes. You can correct them later.

Revising   Be Sure It Makes Sense

▶ **Ideas** Do your characters act real?

▶ Could your setting be a real place?

▶ Could the events in your story really happen?

Editing/Proofreading   Look Closely at the Details

▶ **Conventions** Check your spelling errors.

▶ Check to make sure proper names and places start with a capital letter.

Publishing   Share Your Story

▶ **Presentation** Make a neatly typed or written final copy.

▶ Draw a picture to go with your story.

Picture Books

A **picture book** has words and pictures. The pictures help tell the story. Picture books are made for young children who are learning to read. Adding pictures helps a reader see more about the story.

Try It!

Can you name a picture book you have read?

Take a Look

Rebecca is making a picture book for her brother. First she made a story map for her ideas.

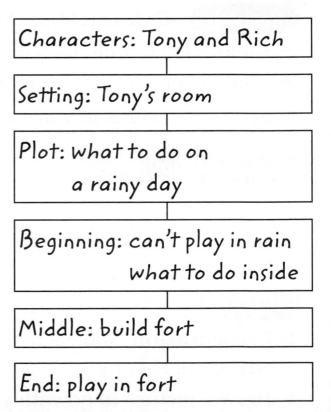

Characters: Tony and Rich

Setting: Tony's room

Plot: what to do on a rainy day

Beginning: can't play in rain what to do inside

Middle: build fort

End: play in fort

Writing a Picture Book

Next she used her notes to write the story.

Rainy Day

Tony and Rich were sad. They wanted to play catch, but it was raining. They sat in Tony's room and tried to think of something to do.

"I know. We can make a fort," said Tony.

"How?" asked Rich.

"We can use cardboard boxes," said Tony. "We can tape the boxes together and draw pictures on them."

The boys got to work. They taped their boxes together and drew on them. When it was done, they went inside it.

"What a great idea!" said Rich.

Adding the Pictures

Rebecca drew three pictures to go with her story.

Tony and Rich were sad. They wanted to play catch, but it was raining. They sat in Tony's room and tried to think of something to do.

"I know. We can make a fort," said Tony.

"How?" asked Rich.

"We can use cardboard boxes," said Tony. "We can tape the boxes together and draw pictures on them."

The boys got to work. They taped their boxes together and drew on them. When the fort was done, they went inside it.

"What a great idea!" said Rich.

Reading Your Writing

When you make a picture book, make sure your pictures match what's going on in the story.

Tips for Making a Picture Book

Prewriting Make a Plan

▶ List topics that interest you or small children.

▶ Pick one idea from your list for your topic.

▶ Plan your story. Use a story map.

Drafting Put Your Thoughts on Paper

▶ Write your story. Use your notes.

▶ Draw pictures that match your story.

Revising Be Sure It Makes Sense

▶ **Ideas** Did you choose an interesting topic?

▶ **Organization** Do you tell the events in order?

▶ Do your pictures match your story?

Editing/Proofreading Look Closely at the Details

▶ **Conventions** Check your spelling.

▶ Make sure you capitalized proper nouns.

Publishing Share Your Story

▶ **Presentation** Make a cover with a picture and title for your story on it.

▶ Read your picture book out loud and show your pictures.

Writing a Fantasy

A **fantasy** is a story in which parts of or all of the story could not happen in the real world.

Parts of a Fantasy

▶ People, animals, or objects are able to do things they cannot do in the real world (a girl shrinks, a teapot talks).

▶ Things happen that could not happen in the real world (rocks turn into gold or time moves faster).

▶ The story takes place in a make-believe place that doesn't exist in the real world (a life-size gingerbread house).

▶ The story has creatures in it that are not found in the real world (dragons, unicorns, or mermaids).

Take a Look

Nicole had to write a fantasy story for homework. Here are Nicole's notes for her fantasy story.

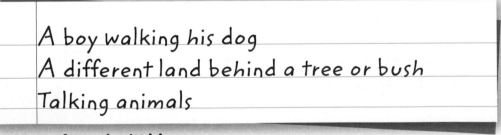

A boy walking his dog
A different land behind a tree or bush
Talking animals

Here is the first part of Nicole's fantasy story.

One day after school, Jasper was taking Scrappy for a walk in the park. Scrappy saw an animal run behind some bushes. Scrappy dragged Jasper to the bushes. They were not in the park anymore! Jasper looked around and saw things he had never seen before. The sky was gold, and the grass was all the colors of the rainbow.

Jasper was so busy looking around that he did not see that Scrappy was standing on two feet instead of all four! Scrappy said, "I don't need this leash now. Please help me take it off." Jasper couldn't believe what was happening!

Reading Your Writing

Make sure your story's events follow some sort of logical order. Watch out for spelling and punctuatioon mistakes.

Tips for Writing a Fantasy Story

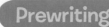 **Prewriting**   Make a Plan

▶ Look for a story in your portfolio that you could make into a fantasy.

▶ Think of which element or elements of fantasy you want to include. Think about how you will include them.

 **Drafting**   Put Your Thoughts on Paper

▶ Write on every other line of your paper so you have space to make changes later.

 Revising   Be Sure It Makes Sense

▶ **Ideas** Have you included fantasy elements in your story?

▶ **Organization** Do you have a good beginning, middle, and end?

▶ **Sentence Fluency** Have you used some long and some short sentences?

▶ **Conventions** Proofread for spelling.

▶ Have you capitalized proper nouns?

Publishing Share Your Work

▶ **Presentation** Write a clean copy of your story, and illustrate it.

▶ Consider turning your story into a puppet show or play.

Fairy Tales

A **fairy tale** is a story that involves imaginary creatures with magical powers, mysterious adventures or occurrences, and a happy ending.

Parts of a Fairy Tale

Here are some things you may find in a fairy tale.

▶ It usually begins with "Once upon a time."

▶ It takes place in a faraway, made-up place.

▶ It has make-believe characters, such as elves, dragons, and giants.

▶ It may have royal characters, such as kings, queens, princes, and princesses.

▶ Things often happen or appear in threes, such as three wishes.

▶ A problem is solved.

▶ It has a happy ending.

Can you think of a fairy tale you have read? Is there one you like best? What about it makes it a fairy tale?

Take a Look

Julie wants to write a fairy tale. She wrote some ideas down in a story map.

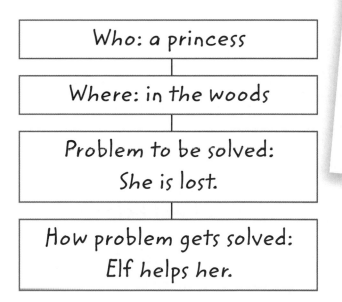

Who: a princess

Where: in the woods

Problem to be solved:
She is lost.

How problem gets solved:
Elf helps her.

Writing a Fairy Tale

Here is the fairy tale Julie wrote using her story map.

The Lost Princess

Beginning ▶
Royalty ▶ Once upon a time, there was a princess named Dorina.

Problem ▶ One day, while Dorina was walking in the woods, she got lost. She sat on a log and thought about what to do.

Make believe creature ▶ All of a sudden, she heard a voice say, "What's wrong, princess?" She looked up and saw a strange little creature. It was an elf with a long gray beard.

"I'm lost," said Dorina.

The elf said, "Follow me. I will help you."

Problem solved ▶ Dorina followed the elf through the woods. She was glad when she saw her
Happy ending ▶ castle. Dorina thanked her new friend. She was happy to be home.

Tips for Writing a Fairy Tale

Prewriting   Make a Plan

▶ Make a list of some make-believe places and things.

▶ Think about some make-believe characters to use. Use a story map to plan your fairy tale.

Drafting   Put Your Thoughts on Paper

▶ Write your fairy tale. Use your notes.

▶ Don't worry about mistakes. You can correct them later.

Revising   Be Sure It Makes Sense

▶ **Ideas** Does your story have parts that make a fairy tale?

▶ **Organization** Does your fairy tale have a problem? Did you solve it?

▶ Does your story have a happy ending?

Editing/Proofreading   Look Closely at the Details

▶ **Conventions** Check your spelling.

▶ Capitalize proper nouns and beginnings of sentences.

Publishing   Share Your Fairy Tale

▶ **Presentation** Make a neatly typed or written final copy.

Action Tales

An **action tale** is a form of narrative writing. It is a story that has a lot of exciting action. All stories have the same parts, which include setting, characters, and plot. In an action tale, the main character has a problem to solve. The story has a lot of action as the character solves the problem.

Take a Look

Julie wants to write an action tale. She plans her story using a story map.

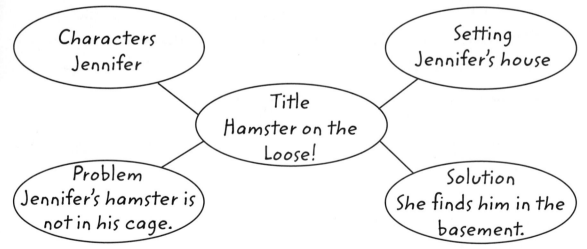

Characters
Jennifer

Setting
Jennifer's house

Title
Hamster on the
Loose!

Problem
Jennifer's hamster is
not in his cage.

Solution
She finds him in the
basement.

Make it Exciting

Next Julie writes ideas for how to use action in her story. She thinks of ways for the problem of the missing hamster to be solved using a lot of action.

Problem

▶ The hamster cage has fallen to the floor.

▶ The cage door has broken and is open.

▶ Julie's room is a mess!

Solution

▶ Julie runs around the room calling for the hamster.

▶ Julie sees her hamster in the basement.

▶ The hamster runs and hides.

▶ Julie gets some food and catches the hamster.

Try It!

Think of how to make each problem and solution have more action.

▶ John wants to borrow a library book, but his library card is gone.

▶ Our teacher has the flu, so we have a substitute teacher today.

▶ Henry is hungry, so he makes a sandwich.

Here is Julie's action tale.

Hamster on the Loose!

Julie came home from school and went to her room. She wanted to say hello to Scooter, her pet hamster. Julie could not believe it! The hamster cage was on the floor. The cage's door was open, and Scooter was not there! Julie ran around her room calling for Scooter. She moved toys and looked under her bed. She opened the closet door and looked inside. But there was no Scooter!

Julie remembered that Scooter loves to play in the basement. She ran down the stairs and turned on the lights. She saw Scooter run and hide behind a chair. Julie tried to pick him up, but she couldn't reach him under the chair. Julie had an idea! She went up the stairs and got some lettuce. Lettuce is Scooter's favorite food. Scooter smelled the lettuce. He came out and climbed on Julie's hand. Now he was safe.

Tips for Writing an Action Tale

Prewriting   Make a Plan

▶ Look for a story in your portfolio to which you could add a lot of action.

Drafting   Put Your Thoughts on Paper

▶ Write on every other line on your paper so you will have space to make changes later.

Revising   Be Sure It Makes Sense

▶ **Ideas** Does your main character have a problem to solve?

▶ **Organization** Does your story follow the order in which the events happened?

Editing/Proofreading   Look Closely at the Details

▶ **Conventions** Proofread for spelling.

Publishing   Share Your Action Tale

▶ **Presentation** Make a clean copy of your story, and illustrate it.

Folktales

A folktale is an old story that teaches a lesson about life. They are told by storytellers and sometimes are not written down. The folktale follows a pattern of repetition in which a similar event occurs over and over with only minor changes.

Parts of a Folktale

Here are some elements you might find in a folktale.

▶ A beginning such as "Once upon a time" or "Long ago and far away"

▶ Characters, such as animals, that can speak

▶ An outcome that affects many characters

▶ A lesson or moral

▶ Written from the third-person point of view (using the words *he*, *she*, or *it* instead of *I*)

▶ Action or words that are frequently repeated

▶ An exciting high point at the end

▶ An outcome where good overcomes evil

FUN FACT

There are still storytellers today. Some people have jobs as storytellers. They travel all over to tell stories and folktales to groups of people.

Jenny wants to write a folktale about how a beaver got its strong, flat tail. She begins by writing a story map about how the beaver's tail became flat.

Title	How the Beaver Got His Flat Tail
Characters	Beaver, Rabbit, Squirrel, Possum, Raccoon, Bear
Setting	Forest
First Problem	A tree lands on and flattens Beaver's tail, and he cannot move. The animals help by digging out Beaver's tail.
Second Problem	Beaver is being chased by Bear.
Outcome	Because of Beaver's new tail, he is able to swim fast, slap water in Bear's face, and escape.
Moral	All beavers have flat tails and can swim very fast.
	If you help others, they are likely to help you.

Student Model

After Jenny organized her ideas, this is what her story looked like.

How Beaver Got His Flat Tail

Once upon a time in a green forest, there lived a beaver. He had a big, bushy tail and strong, sharp teeth. He helped other animals. One stormy day, Raccoon was getting wet. Beaver offered to build her a shelter. He found a tree and took a bite. Chomp, chomp, chomp. He worked in the rain. Chomp, chomp, chomp. Then, BOOM! The tree was lit by lightening and it caught on fire. It started to fall. Beaver ran away but he was not fast enough. The tree landed on his tail! Raccoon saw him and helped pull him out. Bear saw what happened and chased Beaver into the water. Bear scared away Raccoon, but now Beaver could swim very fast with his new flat tail!

Tips for Writing a Folktale

Prewriting   Make a Plan

▶ Plan and organize the plot using a story map.

Drafting   Put Your Thoughts on Paper

▶ Don't stray from the main point of the folktale.

Revising   Be Sure It Makes Sense

▶ **Ideas** Is the life lesson clear in my folktale?

▶ **Organization** Do I include only those details that help show the folktale's lesson?

▶ **Voice** Do I make my characters speak in a way that makes sense in the story?

▶ **Word Choice** Do my words describe the moods and feelings of my characters well?

▶ **Sentence Fluency** Do my sentences help readers move from one point to the next?

Editing/Proofreading   Look Closely at the Details

▶ **Conventions** Make sure end marks are used correctly.

Publishing   Share Your Folktale

▶ Decide whether you want to illustrate your folktale.

Plays

A **play** is a story that is written for actors to perform on stage in front of an audience. It is a story we see and hear instead of read. The author is called a playwright.

Writing a Play

A play has **stage directions, lines** and **props.**

Stage Directions

Stage directions are the directions that tell the actor what to do on stage. They are written in parentheses so the actor knows not to speak those words but just to follow the directions in the words.

Example: *(George Washington stands outside the door of Betsy Ross's home and knocks on her door. There are sounds of horses walking in the background.)*

Lines

Lines tell the actor what to say. A writer will put the name of the character at the beginning of the line in all capital letters followed by a colon. This indicates who is speaking. Example:

BETSY ROSS: Good afternoon, Mr. Washington. It is good to see you today.

Props

Props are things the actor uses on stage, clothing the actor wears (also called costumes), and sound effects made offstage.

Example: Sounds of horses, a large door, two soft chairs for MS. ROSS and MR. WASHINGTON to sit on, and clothing worn by colonists

Student Model

Here is part of the play that Bob wrote about Jack and the Beanstalk.

Characters:	JACK
	MOTHER
	BUTCHER

Time: Long, long ago

Place: Country outside large kingdom

Props: cow costume, beans

MOTHER: Oh Jack, my poor boy. We have nothing left to eat, and our cow no longer gives milk. You will need to take her to town to sell her so we can get money to buy food.

JACK: Yes, Mother.

(JACK walks to town)

BUTCHER: Hello, young boy. Where are you going with that cow?

JACK: I am going into town to sell her.

BUTCHER: Well, my boy, I have five beans that I will give you for your cow.

JACK: My mother and I need to eat, sir. Five beans will not be enough.

BUTCHER: They are magic beans.

JACK: Okay, I hope you are right.

(JACK gives the BUTCHER the cow and takes the beans home to his MOTHER)

continued . . .

Reading Your Writing

As you write your play, be sure the lines and stage directions make sense because the play will be acted out by other people.

Tips for Writing a Play

Prewriting   **Make a Plan**

▶ Choose a story you already know.

▶ Develop your stage directions and dialogue based on what you want to happen in your play.

Drafting   **Put Your Thoughts on Paper**

▶ Write what each character in your play will say.

▶ Add stage directions.

Revising   **Be Sure It Makes Sense**

▶ **Ideas** Did you include the most important events from the story?

▶ **Organization** Do your stage directions go with the action that is taking place?

Editing/Proofreading   **Look Closely at the Details**

▶ **Conventions** Did you remember to put the characters' names at the beginning of their lines?

▶ Did you put parentheses around the stage directions?

Publishing   **Share Your Play**

▶ Write a neat copy of your play. Make a cover with the name of the play on it.

▶ Practice and perform your play. Use real people and costumes or puppets.

Forms of Writing

Descriptive Writing

Descriptive writing gives a clear picture to your readers. It helps your readers see what you see. It helps them hear what you hear. It helps them feel what you feel. The following lesson will give you tips on writing good descriptions.

Writing Descriptions

Descriptions are words that make a picture in a reader's mind. The pictures can be of people, places, things, or actions. Description words help the reader see, hear, smell, taste, and feel things the writer tells them.

Try It!

Here are some examples of description words. Can you think of some more?

soft sweater **blue** sky

loud music **sour** pickle

Take a Look

Jennifer wanted to enter a writing contest. She decided to write a description. First she chose a topic she could write about using description words. Then she used a web to organize her ideas.

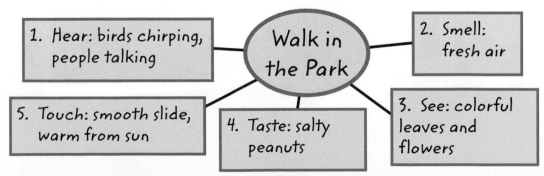

1. Hear: birds chirping, people talking

Walk in the Park

2. Smell: fresh air

5. Touch: smooth slide, warm from sun

4. Taste: salty peanuts

3. See: colorful leaves and flowers

Take a Look

Here's the descriptive paragraph that Jennifer wrote. She used the web to help her.

A Walk in the Park

Mom and I took a walk in the park. We heard birds chirping and people talking. We smelled the fresh air. We saw green leaves and red flowers. We got some peanuts. They tasted salty. At the playground, the slide was smooth and warm from the sun. I love to walk in the park.

FUNFACT

The game "I Spy" is just a describing activity.

Reading Your Writing

Using description words helps your reader better understand your writing. Make sure to use words that help the reader see, hear, feel, smell, or taste things you write about.

Tips for Writing a Description

Make a Plan

▶ List some things you could describe.

▶ Use a web to write details that you can see, hear, smell, taste, or feel.

▶ Pick one idea from your list for your topic.

Put Your Thoughts on Paper

▶ Write your description. Use your web.

▶ Don't worry about mistakes. You can correct them later.

Be Sure It Makes Sense

▶ **Ideas** Did you choose something that can be described?

▶ **Word Choice** Did you use good describing words?

▶ **Organization** Do you have a topic sentence for your paragraph?

Editing/Proofreading **Look Closely at the Details**

▶ **Conventions** Did you indent your paragraph?

▶ Did you check your spelling?

▶ Did you use capital letters for proper nouns and the beginnings of sentences?

Publishing **Share Your Paragraph**

▶ **Presentation** Make a neatly typed or written final copy.

▶ Add drawings or pictures.

Comparing and Contrasting

When you **compare** objects, you talk about how they are *alike*. When you **contrast** objects, you talk about how they are *different*. Writers use clue words to let you know whether they are comparing or contrasting items. Some comparing clue words are *both*, *same*, *like*, *as*, and *too*. Some contrasting clue words are *different* and *but*.

Try It!

Which sentence compares two objects? Which sentence contrasts two objects?

1. Apples and oranges are fruits.
2. Apples are red, but oranges are orange.

Writing to Compare and Contrast Objects

▶ First Paragraph: Begin with a topic sentence to introduce the two subjects. Describe the ways they are alike. Use clue words such as *both*, *also*, *too*, and *as well*.

▶ Second Paragraph: Begin with a sentence that tells readers how the subjects are different. Describe the differences using clue words such as *but*, *unlike*, *however*, and *different*.

Here is a comparison that Tyler wrote.

Apples and Oranges

Apples and oranges are the same in many ways. Apples and oranges are both fruits. Apples grow on trees, and oranges do too. You can find seeds in an apple as well as in an orange. Apples and oranges are good for you.

Apples and oranges are different in many ways. They are different colors. Apples can be red, green, or yellow, but oranges are always orange. The skin of apples and oranges are different because you can eat the skin of an apple. You cannot eat the skin of an orange. Finally, apples and oranges taste different.

Reading Your Writing

Including clue words will help your reader understand your writing. Make sure you use clue words to compare and contrast your subjects.

Forms of Writing

Persuasive Writing

Persuasive writing does two things. It can make readers think or feel a certain way. It can also make readers do something. Sometimes persuasive writing can do both of these things at the same time. Advertisements are one kind of persuasive writing.

You will learn about other kinds in the lessons that follow.

Writing to Persuade

One way to persuade your reader to think or act a certain way is to give good reasons.

Try It!

Below are two good reasons to get someone to study. Can you think of another good reason?

▶ It helps you learn.
▶ It helps you get good grades.

You can write a persuasive paragraph. First think about what you might want to persuade others to do. That will be your topic. Then write down some reasons.

Take a Look

Jeff wants to persuade his parents to get a dog.

1. Will feed — Get a dog — 2. Take it for walks — 3. Help buy with allowance

Here's the sample persuasive paragraph that Jeff wrote.

Getting a Dog

Our family should get a dog. I will offer some of my allowance to help buy one. I will feed it every day. On Saturdays I will take it for a walk. It will help guard our house and keep us safe. I think a dog would be a great pet for our family.

Reading Your Writing

Make sure you support your topic with good reasons. They will help you show that your topic makes good sense.

Tips for Writing a Persuasive Paragraph

Prewriting Make a Plan

▶ What are some things you want to persuade others to do?

▶ Make a list.

▶ Who will you be trying to persuade?

▶ List some reasons that will persuade your audience.

▶ Put your ideas in a web.

Drafting Put Your Thoughts on Paper

▶ Write your paragraph. Use your web from prewriting.

▶ Don't worry about mistakes. You can correct them later.

Revising   **Be Sure It Makes Sense**

▶ **Ideas** Does your topic persuade others to do something?

▶ Do you have good reasons to support your topic?

▶ **Organization** Did you write your topic in the first sentence?

▶ **Sentence Fluency** Are all your sentences complete? Are they easy to read?

Editing/Proofreading   **Look Closely at the Details**

▶ **Conventions** Check for spelling errors.

▶ Make sure proper names and beginnings of sentences start with a capital letter.

Publishing   **Share Your Paragraph**

▶ **Presentation** Make a neatly typed or written final copy.

▶ Draw a picture to go with your paragraph.

Posters

A **poster** is a big sign. Posters are a way to share information with people. Some posters try to persuade. Posters are often bright and colorful.

Take a Look

Here is a poster Anne made for her school. She wants to persuade others to visit the zoo.

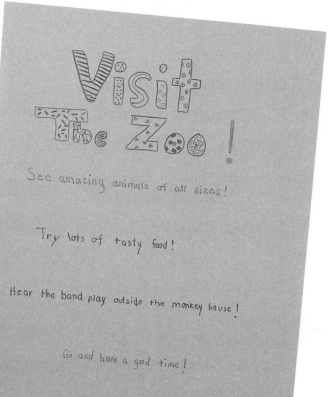

Try It! Find the words Anne used in her poster to tell people what they might see, taste, and hear at the zoo.

Posters

Some posters use feelings to tell something. These posters try to get people to think or act a certain way.

Take a Look

Adam wants his school to recycle. Here is the poster he made for his classmates and teachers.

Reading Your Writing

Making a poster is a great way to share information with others. You can also make a poster to persuade others to do something. Posters are often bright and colorful, so be creative!

Forms of Writing

Poetry

Poetry is very different from other kinds of writing. Think of some poems you have read. They look very different from stories or articles. There is something else about poetry. It can describe things in a way that you may never have thought about before. The lessons on the following pages will show you how to write some different kinds of poetry.

Rhyming Poetry

Poetry joins the sound and meaning of words to create ideas and feelings.

Poetry is not like other kinds of writing. Below are some examples of what makes poetry special.

▶ Sentences are sometimes broken into parts.

▶ Words that rhyme are often used.

▶ The lines of a poem often have rhythm.

In rhyming poetry the last word in a line rhymes with the last word in another line. Here are some examples of rhyming poetry.

In the example below, the first two lines rhyme, and the last two lines rhyme.

My Best Friend

I have a friend named Sunny.
She makes me laugh. She's funny.
She likes to play board games with me,
And friends we will always be.

More Rhyming Poetry

Here is an example of a poem with three lines. All three lines rhyme.

> Flying Balloons
> My balloon sailed up in the sky.
> It made me say, "Oh my!"
> Then it began to fly.

Here is an example of a poem with four lines. Every other line rhymes.

> Little Lost Dog
> There was a little dog named Star
> Who liked to run all day.
> But often times he'd run too far
> And then he'd lose his way.

Try It!

Can you think of other rhyming words that would fit into the poem above?

Reading Your Writing

Poetry is a great way to entertain your readers. You can write your own rhyming poems with two, three, or four lines.

Nonrhyming Poetry

In **nonrhyming** poetry, the last word in each line does not rhyme. There are many different types of nonrhyming poetry.

Acrostics

Acrostics are poems that use letters of a word or name to begin each line.

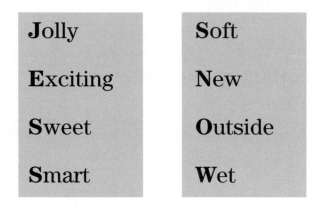

Jolly

Exciting

Sweet

Smart

Soft

New

Outside

Wet

Roses are red
Violets are
Blue

Shape Poems

In a **shape poem** words are put together to form a picture. The picture is something in the poem.

My fish is green and red.
He swims
back and
forth.
His name is Fred.

Free-Verse Poems

A **free-verse** poem does not rhyme or have a pattern.

I ride my bike to school.
I see colors on the way.
I love autumn!

Pattern Poetry

Some poetry follows a pattern. Some poems have both length and rhyming patterns. These poems sound like a poem or song you know, but the words are different.

Take a Look

Here is a poem you all know.

Row, row, row your boat
Gently down the stream.
Merrily, merrily, merrily, merrily,
Life is but a dream.

Here is the pattern poem that Alissa wrote using the poem "Row, Row, Row Your Boat."

Ride, ride, ride your bike
Safely down the street.
Carefully, carefully, carefully, carefully,
Bikes are such a treat.

Can you think of a short poem or song you like? Try to think of some new words for it.

Reading Your Writing

Pattern poems sound like poems and songs you know. Pattern poems can be fun to write and read. Remember that these poems have the same patterns as other poems, but the words are different.

A **riddle poem** is a type of nonrhyming poem. The last word in each line does not rhyme.

Carmen wants to write a riddle poem. She begins with the topic of her poem. The topic is also the answer to the riddle. She will write about flowers. Carmen creates the following list of words and phrases to describe flowers.

colorful
spring
scented
different types
plant in ground
on a stem
pretty to look at

Try It! Think of an object to use as the answer to a riddle. How would you describe this object? How does it feel? How does it taste? How does it smell? Where would you find it?

Student Model

Here is Carmen's riddle poem.

I come in many different colors.
I have many different types.
I smell pretty.
You can put me in the ground.
I grow on a stem.
You can see me in spring.

What am I? a flower

Reading Your Writing

Concrete objects such as bananas and dogs are easier to use in a riddle poem than topics such as bravery and fear. Make sure to use descriptive words in your poem to create a picture in the reader's mind. It is also important that your clues are clear and easy to understand.

Forms of Writing

Writing on Demand

Having to complete a writing assignment in a certain amount of time teaches you to organize your writing and follow directions. Underlining parts of the directions helps you understand the assignment. Making notes about your subject helps you organize your ideas and plan your writing. Then later you can go back and add to your writing. Good luck!

Writing on Demand Strategies

Writing on Demand assignments require you to write about a topic in a specific amount of time. There are strategies that will help you complete a writing on demand assignment.

Writing on Demand Strategies

▶ Read the entire writing prompt. Circle the directions for writing the paper, and underline each thing you are asked to write about. Read through each reminder.

▶ Take a few minutes to make notes about your subject.

▶ Write your paper.

▶ Check you work. Did you respond to each reminder?

▶ Revise as needed.

Lily read the writing prompt for a timed writing assignment.

Write a paragraph about your first day of second grade. How did you feel? What did you do?

Use the writing on demand strategies to help Lily get ready to write her paper. What does she need to do?

Take a Look

Here is the paragraph Lily wrote.

I am in second grade this year. I was scared on the first day of school. I did not know if any of my friends would be in my class. Also, I had not met my teacher yet. Once I walked into my classroom, I felt much better. My friends Jennifer and Allison were in my class! My teacher, Mrs. White, was so nice. She smiled a lot. It was a great first day of school.

Should Lily change anything about her writing? Which strategy did she forget to use?

Narrative Writing

Read the following writing prompt:

Have you ever been on a vacation? Write about your vacation. Where did you go? What did you do? Who was with you? If you have not been on a vacation, *imagine* where you would like to go, what you would do, and who would go with you.

▶ Do you understand the assignment?

▶ Did you circle the important reminders?

Next make notes about your subject:

—Where did I go? Myrtle Beach

—Who was with me? Mom, Dad, and little sister

—What did I do? saw the ocean, built a sandcastle, collected seashells, tried crab cake at dinner

Narrative Writing

Now use your notes to write a story about what happened on your vacation.

My Vacation at the Beach

Last summer my family went to Myrtle Beach. Mom, Dad, my little sister, and I drove from our house to South Carolina. We stayed at a beautiful hotel right on the beach. Every day we went to the beach to enjoy the sunshine and the ocean. It was so much fun to splash in the waves. My sister and I built a sandcastle that we decorated with seashells. We also collected many seashells and kept them in a bucket to take home. Going out to dinner every night was another fun thing we did. Myrtle Beach has a lot of seafood restaurants. I even tried a crab cake. It was delicious! All these activities made the week go by so fast, and soon it was time to head home. We drove back to our house. The first thing I did when I got home was to put the seashell collection in my room. Now I feel like I have a little part of the beach right here at home.

▶ Remember to check your work and make corrections as needed.

Summary Writing

Read the following writing prompt:

> Read the Science Link on **Student Reader,** Book 2 pages 156–157. As you read, you may take notes. After reading the link, write a summary of what you have read. You will have time to read, plan, write, and proofread. You may reread or go back to the article at any time.

▶ Do you understand the assignment?

▶ Did you circle the important reminders?

Next make notes about your subject:

▶ A butterfly has many life stages.

▶ It begins as a tiny egg.

▶ Then a larva forms, and it becomes a caterpillar.

▶ The caterpillar eats for two weeks and grows.

▶ The caterpillar sheds its skin.

▶ The caterpillar attaches to a twig, and its skin splits open again.

▶ It is now a pupa, and it becomes a butterfly.

Summary Writing

Now use your notes to explain the life stages of a butterfly.

Life Stages of a Butterfly

A butterfly has many life stages. First it begins as a tiny egg. Inside the egg, a larva forms, and then it becomes a caterpillar. The caterpillar eats leaves for two weeks and grows. The caterpillar grows so big that it must shed its skin and get bigger skin. Then the caterpillar attaches itself to a twig and sheds its skin again. Now the caterpillar is a pupa. Finally the pupa becomes a butterfly.

▶ Remember to check your work and make corrections as needed.

Quick Write

A **quick write** is when you write your thoughts and ideas about a story in a short amount of time. When quick writing, you do not have to pay too much attention to grammar, spelling, or punctuation. Just write the words, phrases, or sentences that come into your head. Quick writing helps you reflect on what you have learned about the characters and events in a story.

Take a Look

Before doing a quick write, Katie takes a minute to jot down ideas about Mouse from *The Lion and the Mouse*.

1. Mouse caught by Lion
2. Begs Lion to let him go
3. Promises to repay Lion
4. Hears Lion roaring
5. Sets lion free

Take a Look

Katie uses her notes to quick write about Mouse.

Mouse repays Lion's kindness in *The Lion and the Mouse* by Michael Morpurgo. One day, Mouse woke Lion from a nap. Mouse begs Lion to let him go. Mouse promises to repay him, and Lion sets him free. Soon after, Mouse hears Lion roaring because he is caught in a net. Mouse gnaws the net and sets Lion free.

Take a Look

Parker does a quick write to help him learn more about the main events in *The Empty Pot*.

In *The Empty Pot* by Demi, the Emperor of China gives flower seeds to the children. The child who does his or her best to grow flowers will be the next Emperor. Ping tries his best but is not able to grow flowers with the Emperor's seeds. He brings his empty pot to the Emperor. All the other children have grown beautiful flowers using different seeds. Ping's honesty is rewarded. He is chosen as the next Emperor.

Writing Strategies

People read what you write. You want them to enjoy your letters, stories, and poems. You want them to learn from your reports and descriptions. You can help them. Here are some ways to make your writing better.

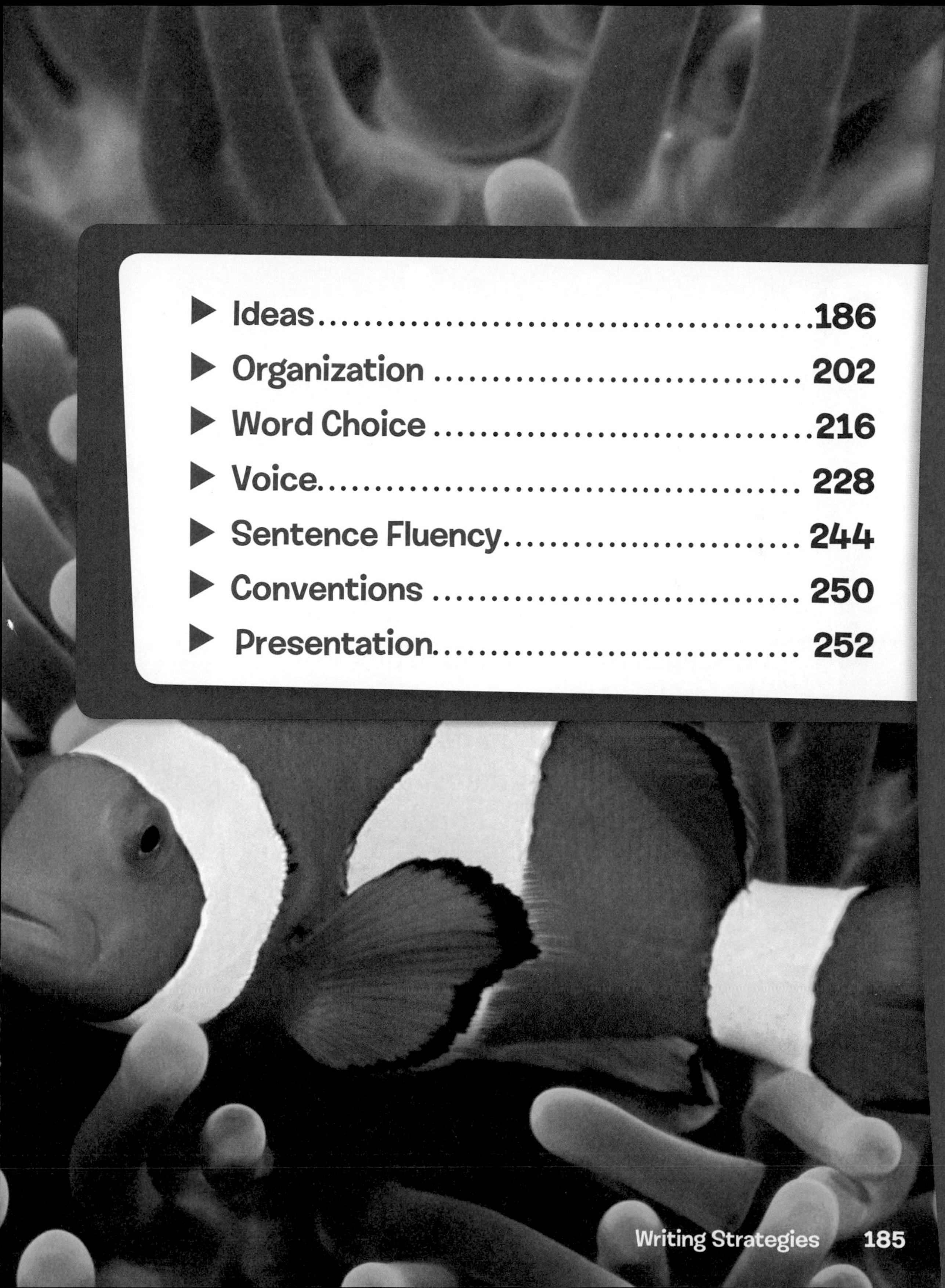

Writing Strategies

Ideas

Ideas are fresh and interesting messages from a writer. They should be clear and easy to read. They should contain many details to support the main idea and should always have correct facts. Ideas should be original and should hold the reader's attention.

Using Drawings to Generate Ideas

Drawing pictures in your writing journal can help remind you of something you want to write about later. **Drawings** can help you remember things that you do not have time to write down.

Take a Look

Ava drew the picture below in her writing journal. Look at her drawing. What do you think Ava will write about based on this drawing? What details will be in her writing? Read her writing on the next page to see whether you were correct.

Here is the paragraph Ava wrote after looking at her drawing.

My Room

My room is my favorite place. I think it is a beautiful room. My mom and dad let me pick out the bedspread. It is white with little purple flowers all over it. I chose it because purple is my favorite color. I also have a vase of purple flowers on my dresser. There's a painting of flowers above my bed. I love all the flowers in my room! I keep my special stuffed bears on my bookshelf. The white bear is Snowflake, and the black bear is Brownie. I also keep some of my books on the bookshelves. I like to sit on my bed and read books at night. My room is a special place for me to be alone. It is also a place for me to keep my things safe. I love spending time in my wonderful room.

Try It!

Draw a picture in your journal of something you would like to write about. Look at your picture later today or tomorrow, and write about it. Was the picture helpful to you? How?

Story Elements

Think of a story you have really enjoyed. Where and when did it take place? What happened? How did you feel about the characters? What did you like most about the story?

Reading stories can be fun. Writing them can be fun, too. Reading lots of stories can help you when you want to write your own story.

Before you begin to write, you need to ask yourself three main questions:

1. Who will be in my story? These are the **characters**.

2. Where and when will the story take place? This is the **setting**.

3. What will happen in the story? What problem will the characters have? How will they solve it? This is the **plot**.

Characters

Characters are the people, animals or imaginary creatures in a story.

Think about these questions.

1. What do my characters look like?

The more details you give about how your characters look, the easier it will be for your readers to picture them.

2. How will my characters act?

Think about what your characters are like. Are they serious, smart, funny, or mean? You decide and then make them talk and act that way in the story.

Some characters may change how they act as the story changes. If they do change, you need to let your reader know why.

3. How will my characters feel?

Show how they feel through the characters' actions and thoughts.

Setting

The **setting** is when and where the story takes place. Describe the setting near the beginning of your story, so your readers can picture when and where your story is happening.

Think about these questions.

1. When does the story take place?

▶ Be exact: yesterday, ten years ago, twenty years from now, Saturday morning, Wednesday at midnight

2. Where does the story take place?

▶ Be exact: the deserts of Arizona, New York City, the top floor of a building, a baseball field, an old house

▶ A story can change settings as things happen. Make sure you tell the readers when the setting changes.

▶ Use sight, sound, and smell words so your reader will be able to clearly picture the setting of your story.

Plot

The **plot** is what happens in a story. The plot usually has a problem that has to be solved. The plot has three parts: the beginning, the middle, and the end.

Beginning: The events at the beginning of the story should tell the problem. The characters and setting are also included in the beginning of your story.

Middle: The characters try to fix the problem during this part. How your story will end is still not told.

Ending: The problem is solved by the characters. How the problem is solved needs to be clear to the reader.

Before you begin to write, think about these things.

▶ What is the problem?

▶ How will the characters deal with the problem?

▶ How will the problem be solved?

Writing Good Beginnings and Endings

A good beginning and ending will make your writing more interesting to read.

Good Beginnings

A good beginning grabs the readers' attention. Here are four ways to start your writing.

▶ Ask a question that will interest the readers.

> What would you do if you found a dinosaur bone in your backyard?
> Would you tell someone or would you keep it a secret?

▶ Tell about a problem.

> Once there was a king who had a beautiful garden. In his garden there was a tree with twelve golden apples. One day the king counted the apples. One was missing.

More Ways to Write Good Beginnings

▶ Use details that describe sight, sound, smell, taste, or touch.

> Tara walked along the hot, dusty road. Her mouth was dry, and she couldn't stop thinking about ice-cold lemonade.

▶ Use dialogue. (Put the speaker's words in quotation marks.)

> "Jason, don't move!" Tad cried. "There's a spider behind you."
>
> "Well, Tad, don't you move either," Jason said slowly. "There's a large bat hanging over your head."

Good Endings

It's important to have a good ending for whatever you write.

Take a Look

Read the ending from a story about a lost dog named Toby.

Toby walked through the dried leaves to the top of a hill. As he got to the top, he heard voices. They were calling, "Toby! Where are you?"

He looked down the hillside and saw his family. Toby's tail began to wag wildly, and he let out a loud bark. Then he raced down the hill to the people who loved him.

Think of something you have written. What kind of beginning did you write? Did your ending tell what happened to your characters?

Reading Your Writing

Your beginning is very important. It gets the audience interested in your story. If your writing doesn't have a good ending, your reader may feel let down and confused.

Adding Details

Details are important when creating the mood of your writing. Adding details to your writing will help readers respond and connect to your ideas. Details describing how something feels, sounds, tastes, or looks are called sensory details. These details can help readers feel like they are part of your writing. Details about characters thoughts and feelings will help readers better understand a story.

Take a Look

Riley wants to write about a trip to the pumpkin patch. She makes a list of sensory details and feelings to use in her writing.

Sensory Details		Feelings/Thoughts
Sights:	pumpkins, scarecrows, leaves	excited hungry
Sounds:	tractor, people	tired
Smells:	popcorn, hot dogs	

Try It!

Think of a place you have visited, and write a list of words to describe how this place looked, smelled, sounded, tasted, and felt. How would you describe your thoughts and feelings while you were at this place?

Here is Riley's writing about her visit to a pumpkin patch.

A Visit to the Pumpkin Patch

I was so excited to go to the pumpkin patch. I had been waiting for the pumpkins to ripen so they could be picked. The pumpkin patch was covered with hundreds of orange dots. Pumpkins were all different shapes and sizes. Scarecrows were around the patch. Some leaves were still hanging on the trees, and others were on the ground. I had fun stepping on the leaves. First I picked up the pumpkin I wanted to take home. It was heavy and smooth with some bumps on it. Next we took a hay ride. The hay tickled my legs as the tractor engine rumbled. I liked the ride. The smell of kettle corn and hot dogs made us hungry, so we ate some. Finally it was time to go home. I was tired from our visit to the pumpkin patch.

Reading Your Writing

Choose a part of your writing to describe with more detail. Add some sensory details, or focus more on a character's thoughts and feelings.

Using Dialogue

Talk or conversation between two or more people in a story is called **dialogue**. You can use dialogue to make your characters seem real.

Take a Look

Using the exact words between characters can be more interesting than just telling about a conversation.

> Daniel whispered to Rachel to pass the peas.
>
> "Can you please pass me the peas?" Daniel whispered.

Why Use Dialogue in Your Writing?

Dialogue can show how the characters feel, which makes them seem more real to the readers. Dialogue makes your audience want to keep reading.

How to Write Dialogue

Quotation marks (" ") are used when writing dialogue. Use quotation marks before and after a character's exact words.

Take a Look

Here is a dialogue that Nick wrote.

"Did you like going to the park?" asked Chip.

"Yes, but I wish we stayed longer," said Randy.

"Next time, let's take a picnic," said Chip.

"That sounds great," said Randy.

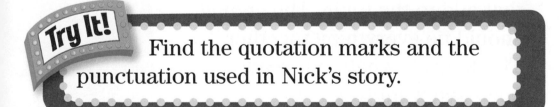

Try It! Find the quotation marks and the punctuation used in Nick's story.

Writing Strategies

Organization

Organization in writing is how you structure the paper. The information should be delivered in a logical way. Good writing begins with good beginnings. The middle should provide details that add to the topic. The ending should tie everything together. Think about what your readers need and want to know.

Graphic Organizers

Graphic organizers are tools that help you plan your writing. They come in different shapes and sizes. *Graphic* means "written or drawn." *Organizer* means "tool for getting your ideas in order."

Webs

Some graphic organizers help you gather ideas to describe something.

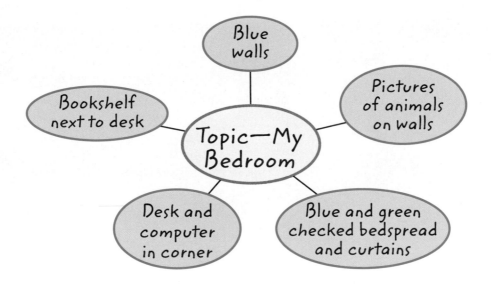

Story Map

Some graphic organizers help you plan a story.

Title	The Poetry Paper

Character	Tonya

Setting	Woods

Plot   Tonya has to write a poem for English.

- Beginning   Tonya can't think of anything to write.

- Middle   Tonya walks in woods instead of writing poem. She sees all kinds of creatures.

- End   Tonya writes poem about things she sees in woods.

Venn Diagram

Some graphic organizers help you compare things.

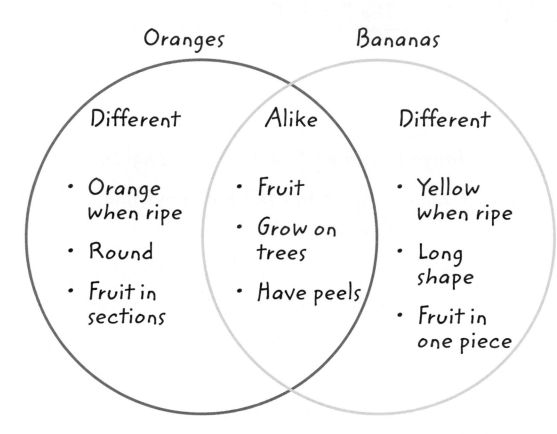

Oranges   Bananas

Different
- Orange when ripe
- Round
- Fruit in sections

Alike
- Fruit
- Grow on trees
- Have peels

Different
- Yellow when ripe
- Long shape
- Fruit in one piece

Try It!

Which graphic organizer would you use for planning to write about each of the ideas below?

▶ describe a puppy
▶ write a story
▶ show how lions and tigers are alike and different

Reading Your Writing

Make a plan before you start writing. It is helpful to collect your ideas in a graphic organizer. When you make a plan, readers will better understand what you write.

Drawing Charts, Time Lines, and Graphs

There are many ways to present information in a visual way. Charts, time lines, and graphs are visual tools that help your audience see important information in a quick and easy way.

Drawings with Labels

Include drawings with labels that name important parts.

Charts

A chart is an easy way to show important information.

Jalisa's First Week of Summer Vacation

DAY	SUNDAY	MONDAY	TUESDAY	WEDNESDAY	THURSDAY	FRIDAY	SATURDAY
ACTIVITY	Fed the fish Went swimming	Fed the fish Read a book	Fed the fish Planted seeds	Fed the fish Went swimming	Fed the fish Helped make a pie	Fed the fish Went to the library	Fed the fish Cleaned my room

Time Lines

Time lines show the order in which events happened.

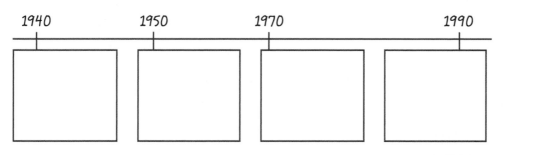

Circle Graph

This graph shows how a whole of something can be divided into parts.

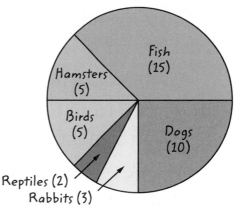

Taking Notes for Writing a Summary

Taking notes from a piece of writing will help you write a summary of it. Record the most important point from each paragraph. Do not copy sentences. Instead, write the most important words or phrases.

Carter read the following paragraph from *Dinosaur Fossils* by Dr. Alvin Granowsky.

We have learned what we know about dinosaurs from their fossils. A fossil is what is left from a plant or animal that lived long ago.

Fossils can be imprints of leaves, shells, eggs, or skeletons. Some fossils are hardened tracks or footprints left by a moving animal.

When a plant or animal dies, it can become covered by many layers of mud and sand. After thousands of years, the bottom layers harden into rock. The dead plant or animal also hardens into rock. This is how fossils are formed.

Here are the notes Carter wrote after reading the article. He wrote down the main points from each paragraph.

from a long time ago
from plants and animals
can be imprints of different things
covered by mud and sand
harden into rock

Carter used his notes to write this summary.

Fossils are left by plants and animals that lived a long time ago. Fossils can be imprints of different things. Sometimes things get covered with mud and sand. Over time, they will harden into rock. This rock is a fossil.

Try It!

Did Carter write down the main points from each paragraph? Should he add anything? Should he take out anything?

Arranging Notes into an Outline

An **outline** is a plan for a piece of writing. You can organize your notes into outlines. You will be able to see the information you have and what you still need to learn. Main topics are listed using Roman numerals. Subtopics are labeled with capital letters.

Here is an example of an outline.

Trees

I. Parts of a Tree
- A. trunk: the main part of a tree that the branches grow out of
- B. limb: a branch of a tree
- C. roots: grow underground and get food from the soil

II. Kinds of Trees
- A. evergreen trees have needle leaves
- B. broadleaf trees have flat, wide leaves

III. Interesting Facts
- A. tell a tree's age by counting number of rings in trunk
- B. absorbs carbon dioxide and gives oxygen

Roman Numerals
1 = I
2 = II
3 = III
4 = IV
5 = V

Take a Look

Tiffany read the notes she wrote while learning about panda bears.

Panda Bears

live in China
found in mountains
black fur on eyes, ears, arms, and legs
white fur coat
eat mostly bamboo
2–3 feet tall
weigh between 220 and 250 pounds
eat grasses and small animals

She organized her notes by writing the main ideas.

Panda Bears

   I. Where They Live
  II. How They Look
 III. What They Eat

Try It!

Now that Tiffany has written the main ideas, help her organize her notes. Where would you put each fact in the outline?

Taking Notes from Guests, Media, and Books

Taking notes allows you to remember the most important information from books, speakers, and media sources. Write down words or phrases to record the main points.

Note-Taking Tips

▶ Write the title or name of where you are getting the information.

▶ Write the date.

▶ Use your own words to write the most important information you learned.

Brenda read the following information from "Animal Camouflage" by Janet McDonnell.

How Do Animals Use Camouflage?

Animals use camouflage in many different ways. Some use it to blend in with the objects around them. These objects are called surroundings. The *polar bear's* white coat blends in with its surroundings—the white snow. This color hides the bear when it is hunting for seals. The *black bear's* dark coat helps it hide in dark trees and bushes.

But what happens if an animal's surroundings are more than one color? Some animals have camouflage with more than one color, too! Some fish have dark backs and white bellies. When a hungry bird looks into the dark water, the fish's dark back is hard to see. But to an enemy deeper in the water, the fish's white belly blends in with the bright sky.

Take a Look

Take a look at the notes Brenda wrote after reading about camouflage.

"Animal Camouflage"
by Janet McDonnell
October 4, 2006

use camouflage in different ways
blend in with surroundings
polar bear and black bear
use more than one color
fish

Try It!

What note-taking tips did Brenda use when writing her notes? Did she include any information that was not important?

Writing Strategies

Word Choice

Good word choices make your writing interesting to read and easy to picture. Use words that help the reader see, feel, and hear your ideas. Carefully choose words that make a lasting impact.

Formality of Language

Formal language is similar to the way you would speak to a teacher, principal, guest speaker, or police officer. Titles such as *Sir, Ma'am, Mr., Mrs.,* and *Miss* are used in formal writing. Careful attention to detail, such as sentence structure and grammar, is very important. Formal writing should be clear and polite.

Business Letter

A business letter is an example of formal writing. People write business letters for many reasons. Here are some examples:

▶ To order or ask for something

▶ To complain about a problem

▶ To ask for information about something

▶ To share opinions and ideas about something

When writing a business letter, you may be writing to someone that you do not know. Remember to use formal language and a polite tone.

Try It!

When would you use formal language? To whom would you write that would make this type of language necessary?

Student Model

Read the letter Cory wrote to a firefighter asking for a classroom visit.

Heading ▶

2511 Hidden Drive
Columbus, OH 43230
September 20, 2006

Inside Address ▶

Mr. Fisher
Columbus Fire Department
300 N. 4th Street
Columbus, OH 43215

Salutation ▶

Dear Mr. Fisher:

Body ▶

My name is Cory Jones. I am in the second grade at Brookview Elementary School. My class will learn about fire safety next month. I know you could teach us a lot of important things. It would also be interesting to hear about your job as a firefighter.

Could you please visit our classroom sometime in the first week of October? We are very excited to meet a real firefighter. I hope to see you soon.

Closing ▶

Signature ▶

Thank you,
Cory Jones

Try It!

What formal language does Cory Jones use in his letter? Is his letter polite and clear?

Action Words

The mood of a story is created by an author's choice of words. Including **action** and **descriptive** words will make a story more exciting. The action in a story is what the characters are doing. Using details to describe the action is even more helpful.

Take a Look

Here is the story Rosita wrote.

Don't Miss the Bus!

I got up late this morning. My alarm clock did not wake me. Mom came into my room and told me that the school bus would be here in ten minutes. I got out of bed and put on my clothes. Then I walked into the bathroom. I brushed my teeth and combed my hair. Finally I went to the kitchen and ate cereal. The bus was waiting at the bus stop. I grabbed my book bag. I got on the bus. Wow! That was a close call. I'm so glad I didn't miss the bus!.

Rosita read her writing and decided to add action and descriptive words. Do you think her story is more exciting now? Why?

Don't Miss the Bus!

The sunshine in my eyes woke me up this morning. My alarm clock was broken and did not wake me. Mom ran into my room and yelled, "The school bus will be here in ten minutes!" I jumped out of bed in a flash and threw on my clothes. Then I quickly ran into the bathroom. In a rush, I brushed my teeth and combed my hair. Finally I flew down the stairs and gobbled down my cereal. The bus was honking its horn at the bus stop. I grabbed my book bag and threw it over my shoulder. I got on the bus just as the doors were closing. Wow!

That was a close call. I'm so relieved I didn't miss the bus!

Reading Your Writing

Choosing your words carefully creates the mood of your story. Make sure your story uses verbs to create action. Ask yourself whether you can change any verbs to make your story more interesting. Including details will make your writing more exciting.

Descriptive Words

An **adjective** is a word that describes a person, place, or thing. In your writing, use adjectives that appeal to the reader's five senses.

The Five Senses

Sight

Some adjectives help readers see in their minds what you are describing.

> The <u>gold</u> and <u>orange</u> leaves fell from the tree.
>
> She hugged her <u>chubby, worn</u> teddy bear.

Smell

Some adjectives help the reader imagine a smell that is being described.

> Did you smell the <u>fresh, sweet</u> flowers?
>
> The air was <u>stale</u> in the old cabin.

Sound

Some adjectives help the reader hear what is happening.

> The <u>gurgling</u> water poured out of the faucet.
>
> The swarm of angry, <u>buzzing</u> bees left the hive.

Taste

Some adjectives help the reader imagine how something tastes.

> He sliced the <u>tart, juicy</u> apples for his pie.
> We shared a bag of <u>salty, crunchy</u> peanuts.

Touch

Some adjectives help your reader imagine how an object feels.

> The <u>prickly</u> shrub scraped my legs.
> Tad picked up the <u>slimy</u> frog.

Try It!

Think about your favorite snack. How could you describe it using adjectives that connect to the five senses?

Writing Connection

Adjectives describe nouns and pronouns. Use adjectives to help readers imagine the sight, smell, sound, taste, or touch of something.

Precise Word Choice

Word Choice is an important part of writing. A writer must carefully choose the best words to help his or her readers create a picture in their mind.

Why Is Word Choice Important?

Choosing good descriptive words will make your ideas clear and your writing enjoyable to read. Words such as *roaring* and *slimy* give readers an exact sense of feeling and sound. Also, interesting verbs, such as *chuckled* and *crawled*, help create that picture in the reader's mind. Below are some words with an example of a more precise word choice.

said	exclaimed
cried	sobbed
sad	heartbroken
ran	dashed

Try It!

Can you think of other examples of better word choices for these words? Think of some other words, and then come up with more descriptive words that could replace them.

Student Model

Read Annie's story.

The Rollercoaster Ride

Tracy had never ridden on a rollercoaster before. The roaring sound of the coaster as it flew on the metal tracks had always frightened her. But today, she was determined to ride a rollercoaster. Tracy marched up to the line and waited her turn. She felt butterflies in her stomach. She tried not to listen to the screams of the other riders. Tracy handed over her ticket and crawled into the seat. Her heart started pounding when she heard the seatbelt click. Slowly, the rollercoaster climbed up the hill. The next two minutes were filled with loops and turns. Tracy was jolted from one side to the other. Her stomach was spinning around. When it stopped, she could not believe it. She loved riding roller coasters!

Try It!

What words in Annie's story helped create a picture in your mind as you read? Did other parts of the story help you do this?

Descriptive Dialogue

Dialogue is a feature writers use to tell the audience what the characters are thinking and feeling. When dialogue is **descriptive** and realistic, it makes characters seem real to the reader. Descriptive dialogue will make your audience want to keep reading.

Take a Look

Read the two examples of dialogue below.

"I think we should go the the park," Peter said.
"That is a good idea," Bobby said.
"Let's have a picnic lunch," Peter said.
"I will bring a ball," Bobby said.

"It is a sunny day without a cloud in the sky.

Let's enjoy the weather at the park!" Peter exclaimed.

"Wow! What an amazing idea!" Bobby cried.

"I'll pack sandwiches, apples, and milk for a picnic lunch," Peter said.

"I'll grab a ball, and we can play catch after we eat," Bobby suggested.

Which example of dialogue makes you want to continue reading? Why?

How Do You Write Descriptive Dialogue?

To make dialogue more descriptive, think about how you talk to other people. You do not talk in choppy, short sentences. You use a lot of detail and excitement when talking to others. Remember this when writing your dialogue.

Try It!

Choose a topic for two characters to discuss. Write some dialogue between the characters. Now discuss this same topic with a friend. How was your conversation different than the written dialogue? Can you think of a way to make the written dialogue more descriptive and realistic?

Reading Your Writing

Using dialogue in a story is more interesting than just telling about a conversation. For dialogue to be descriptive, it must seem like a real conversation. Think about how the characters feel, and try to use words that will show the feelings in the dialogue.

Writing Strategies

Voice

Voice is the way the writer tells the story to the reader. It shows the writer's personality. A strong voice helps the reader feel like a real person is telling them the story.

Audience and Purpose

There are two important questions to ask yourself before you begin any writing.

1. Who will read my writing?

2. What is my reason for writing?

The answers will help you to plan your writing in a clear way.

Audience

Your audience is who you think will read your writing. Knowing your audience helps you think about what your readers want to know.

Purpose

The reason you are writing is your purpose. There are four main purposes for writing.

1. inform or tell about something

2. explain or tell how to do something

3. entertain or amuse

4. persuade people to think or do something

Writing to Inform

When you are writing to inform, you are giving information about a subject. It's important to think about your audience. What might your audience already know? What does your audience need to know?

Take a Look

Matlin wrote about the first airplane flight.

The First Flight

On December 17, 1903, Wilbur and Orville Wright flew an airplane in Kitty Hawk, North Carolina. The plane stayed in the air for twelve seconds. The plane flew about 118 feet. The brothers had been trying to fly since 1896.

Writing to Explain

Another purpose for writing is to explain how to make or do something, or how something works. Think about your audience. How much do you need to explain? Be sure to include all the information your audience needs.

Take a Look

Cortland wrote about how to wash the dishes. His audience was his classmates.

How to Wash Dishes
1. Fill the sink with hot, soapy water.
2. Get a clean dishcloth.
3. Wash and rinse the glasses first.
4. Wash and rinse the silverware next.
5. Then wash the plates.
6. Wash and rinse the greasy pots and pans last.
7. Put everything in a rack to dry, or dry with a towel.

Writing to Entertain

When you write to entertain, think about what your readers would enjoy reading or what would amuse them. There are many ways to entertain others.

▶ stories
▶ poems
▶ descriptions
▶ plays
▶ comic strips

Take a Look

Look at Isaac's journal entry.

A Day in the Life of a Sock

Today, as I was sleeping in the deep, dark drawer of the dresser, Tim yanked me out into the bright morning light. He put me on his VERY cold feet. I was walked on all day. First we went to school. Then we went to a scout meeting. After that, we played in the yard! I really had a busy day!

Writing to Persuade

Writing to persuade is when a writer tries to get readers to think, feel, or act a certain way. You need to know who your audience is and what matters to your audience. Then you can figure out what reasons will persuade them.

Take a Look

Kelly wrote a letter to persuade her principal to let the students visit the zoo.

Dear Ms. Hanson,

Many of the students at this school would like to be able to visit the zoo. There are many reasons this would be a good idea.
1. The zoo makes learning about animals fun.
2. We get to meet other students.
3. All the walking at the zoo is great exercise.
Sincerely,
Kelly

Try It!

Can you think of a topic for each purpose for writing? Who would be your audience for each one?

Reading Your Writing

If you don't think of the purpose and your audience before you plan, your writing will not be as clear as it can be.

Staying on the Topic

A good way to stay on the topic, or main idea, is to make a prewriting plan. Make a web or map for your ideas. Then use your prewriting notes while you write.

Take a Look

Carmine wrote a paragraph about farm animals. He wrote a prewriting plan, but he forgot to check it as he was writing.

Farms can have lots of different kinds of animals. Some farms have cows. Drinking milk is very important to farmers. Some have chickens for their eggs. I like scrambled eggs. Lots of farmers have cats and dogs. Some dogs and cats don't get along very well. A farm can be a home for many different animals.

Try It! How many places can you find in Carmine's paragraph where he got off the topic?

Take a Look

Carmine revised his writing to make sure it stayed on the topic. Read it and compare it to his first paragraph.

Farms can have lots of different kinds of animals. Some farms have cows for milk. Some have chickens for eggs. Lots of farms have cats and dogs. A farm can be a home for many different animals.

Reading Your Writing

If you don't stay on the topic, you will confuse your readers. Using a web or map will help you stay on the topic.

Identifying the Best Feature of Writing

Many different features make good writing. Sometimes it is difficult to choose the best feature. When you think about what it is you like best about your writing, consider some of the following traits.

Ideas

▶ The writing is clear and easy to read. It says something interesting. It includes many details and correct facts.

Organization

▶ The writing piece begins with a good opening. The information is in order. The main idea is presented in an interesting way.

Voice

▶ The writer's personality comes through in the voice he or she uses in the writing. Readers feel like they get to know the writer.

Word Choice

▶ Good word choices paint a picture with words. The words make the writing easy to read and easy to picture in your mind.

Sentence Fluency

All sentences stay on topic. The reader can easily understand the writing.

Conventions

▶ Correct spelling, grammar, punctuation, and capitalization are used. There are no mistakes to confuse readers.

Story Elements

▶ The characters have unique traits. The setting is an important part of the story. The plot is exciting, easy to understand, and the problems are resolved at the end of the story.

▶ A particular part of the story creates a strong emotion, such as sadness, fear, humor, or excitement.

Presentation

▶ The story is written or typed neatly. Pictures and drawing add to the writing. There are interesting visual aids in the story's presentation.

Evaluating Whether Prewriting Purpose Is Met

Often, the first step in planning a piece of writing is deciding on the **purpose** of your writing. The purpose is why you are writing something and what you would like your writing to do.

There are many different writing purposes. Here are a few examples:

▶ To entertain
▶ To inform
▶ To persuade
▶ To remember things
▶ To keep in touch with others

Has the Purpose Been Met?

Understanding your purpose for writing before you start is important. The purpose will focus your ideas and guide your writing. When you go back and read your writing, ask yourself whether your writing does what you wanted it to do. Did you meet the purpose?

Types of Writing

The purpose of your writing will help you decide what kind of writing to use. Look at the following purposes and examples of writing.

Entertain
▶ poem

Inform
▶ summary

Persuade
▶ poster

Remember Things
▶ to-do list

Record Information
▶ learning log

Keep in Touch
▶ friendly letter

Try It!

Can you think of other types of writing for each purpose listed above? What are some other writing purposes and types of writing that would help meet these purposes?

Each student below has a purpose they want to meet in a piece of writing. Read each student's purpose. Can you think of a type of writing that would be a good choice for each student?

1. Georgina wants to thank her Aunt Betty for taking her to the zoo.

2. Stephon wants to tell people about goldfish.

3. Terrance wants to make people laugh.

Georgina wants to thank her Aunt Betty for taking her to the zoo. She wrote a thank-you letter.

Dear Aunt Betty,

Thank you for taking me to the zoo last week. It was so nice of you. I had a great time seeing all the animals. I think the giraffes and zebras were my favorite. I also enjoyed having a picnic lunch with you. It was a wonderful day.

Love,
Georgina

Stephon wants to tell people about goldfish. He wrote a report on goldfish.

Goldfish

Goldfish are the most common household pet. Goldfish are able to get used to different temperatures, food, and types of water. Special food can be purchased at a pet store. Goldfish like to be with other goldfish. Putting three or more goldfish in one bowl is a good idea.

Terrance wants to make people laugh. He wrote a fairy tale.

Once upon a time, there lived a handsome prince. He was fishing one day when he caught a talking fish! "Put me back in the water now!"the fish said and hit the prince's nose with his tail. The prince was angry and put the fish in a bowl of water. He took the fish back to the castle. As punishment, he made the fish tell him a joke every day.
One day, the fish said, "Knock, knock."
The prince replied, "Who's there?"
"Canoe," answered the fish.
"Canoe who?" asked the prince.
"Can you please let me go?"
The prince laughed so hard, he decided to set the fish free. Everyone lived happily ever after.

Writing Strategies

Sentence Fluency

Sentence fluency is the ability to use sentences to create a sense of rhythm. Use long sentences when it makes sense to do so, and include short sentences to break them up. This will create a flow that readers will enjoy.

Varying Sentence Beginnings

Each sentence in a piece of writing should begin a different way. When you **vary sentence beginnings,** your writing will be more interesting to read.

Take a Look

Read the following sentences.

I have a new pair of roller skates. I got them for my birthday. I have always wanted to try roller skates. I use my skates every day.

Now read the sentences after the beginnings have been changed.

I was given a new pair of roller skates. My grandmother gave them to me as a birthday present. Roller skates are something that I have always wanted to try. Every day I am outside using my roller skates.

Which set of sentences is more interesting to read? Why?

Read Brittany's paragraph below. Pay attention to the beginning of her sentences.

Playing at the Park

I love to play at the park. I love to go to the park with my family. I love to swing. I love to slide. I love to have picnics at the park. I know how to climb on the jungle gym. I know how to play hopscotch. It is fun to ride bikes on the bike trails. It is fun to feed the ducks in the pond. It is fun to go to the park.

What problems do you see in Brittany's writing? How would you change her paragraph? How would these changes make her writing better?

Reading Your Writing

Make sure your sentence beginnings vary. Your sentences should flow together and tell a story. You do not want your writing to seem like a list of ideas.

Kinds of Sentences

A **declarative** sentence tells something. It ends with a period (.).

> George Washington was the first U.S. President.

An **interrogative** sentence asks something. It ends with a question mark (?).

> How was your history test?

An **exclamatory** sentence shows strong feeling about something. It ends with an exclamation point (!).

> Wow, that is a huge spider!

An **imperative** sentence gives a command. It ends with a period (.).

Look at this brown spider.

Try It!

What kind of sentences are these?
What time is it?
Close the door, please.
Dogs bark, jump, and play.

Reading Your Writing

Use different types of sentences when you write. You can use declarative, interrogative, exclamatory, or imperative sentences. Be sure to use the correct end mark.

Writing Strategies

Conventions

Conventions are the rules writers follow to make their words and ideas easy to read and understand. Spelling, punctuation, capitalization, grammar, and paragraph structure create organization to guide the reader. Writing that has mistakes may confuse readers. Using conventions correctly is important for a smooth read.

Using Writing Conventions

Remember to check for the following conventions before presenting a piece of writing.

Conventions Checklist

1. Did I spell all the words correctly?

2. Did I use commas, colons, and apostrophes correctly? Did I remember to end each sentence with appropriate end punctuation?

3. Did I capitalize the first word in each sentence? Did I capitalize all the proper nouns?

4. Did I check for grammatical errors? Do all my subjects and verbs agree? Are all my sentences complete?

5. Is my paragraph easy for my reader to understand? Does it follow a logical sequence? Did I use the same tense throughout the paragraph? Did I stay on topic? Did I vary how my sentences begin?

Writing Strategies

Presentation

When you publish your work, you should always make a clean and neat draft. You can add pictures, drawings, graphics, or clip art to make it look better. It is important to show care for the way you present your hard work!

Using Multimedia Sources to Illustrate

Using different **multimedia sources** to illustrate ideas is a useful tool in writing. Visual aids will help your readers better understand the ideas and information in your writing.

Photographs

Photographs provide a realistic view of your topic and ideas. You can use a photograph you take yourself if possible. Scanning photographs from books is

another option. Magazines are another resource in which to find the photographs you need.

Drawings

Drawings are a useful way to illustrate your writing. You will be able to design your drawing to help readers understand your main points. Drawings may be small to accompany a piece of writing. They also may be large posters if you are presenting your ideas to a group of people.

Charts and Graphs

Creating a chart or graph to show facts and figures is very helpful. You can draw a chart or graph. You also can use a computer to create this type of media.

Maps

Maps can help readers visualize an idea presented in a piece of writing. You can draw a map, use a copier to make a print and add your own information, or scan a map onto the computer.

Video Camera

A video camera can be used to capture footage that is related to your topic. You could perform commercials, news reports, plays, or other ideas to illustrate your main points.

Try It!

Which type of media would be helpful to illustrate ideas for each topic?
- ▶ An informative report on snakes
- ▶ Directions to the library
- ▶ A list of favorite colors
- ▶ A play about a wicked queen
- ▶ A newspaper article about school lunches

Vocabulary

Each word has its own meaning. Writers carefully choose the words they use. They want words to communicate exactly what they want to say. When that happens, their writing comes alive for readers. You can make the same choices when you write. Learning about different kinds of words will help.

Making Comparisons

Writers compare one thing to another to help the reader picture things. When you compare, you show how two things are alike in some way. There are many ways you can compare two things.

Similes

A **simile** compares two unlike things using the words *like* or *as*.

Dyan Sheldon uses similes in her story "The Whale's Song." She compares the size of the whales to the size of mountains. She compares the sound of their voices to the sound of the wind.

In her dreams she saw them, <u>as large as mountains</u> and bluer than the sky. In her dreams she heard them singing, <u>their voices like the wind.</u>

Metaphors

A **metaphor** usually says that one thing is another thing. It does this without using *like* or *as*. What is the snow being compared to in this sentence?

The <u>snow is a soft, thick blanket</u> over the city.

Personification

Personification is a kind of metaphor. Nonhuman things are given qualities or actions of human beings.

The <u>trees danced</u> in the wind.

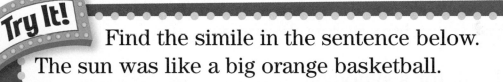

Try It!   Find the simile in the sentence below.
The sun was like a big orange basketball.

Reading Your Writing

When you use similes, metaphors, and personification, your readers can imagine a picture of what you are writing.

Context Clues

When you come across a word in your reading that you do not know, what do you do? One way to figure out the meaning of a new word is to use context clues. **Context clues** are found in other information near the new word.

How to Use Context Clues

Here are a few ways you can use context clues to figure out the meaning of a new word.

1. Look at other sentences for a definition or explanation of the word.

> The human body is an amazing <u>organism</u>. **An organism is any living thing.**

2. Look for a synonym.

> Tara looked <u>agitated</u>, **or nervous,** when she gave her speech.

3. Look for an antonym.

> The dancer was very <u>graceful</u>, **not clumsy,** as he glided across the stage.

Try It!

Use context clues to figure out the meaning of the underlined word in each sentence below.

▶ An adjective <u>modifies</u>, or describes, a noun or pronoun.

▶ There was an <u>error</u>, or mistake, on my paper.

▶ The cloth was <u>moist</u>, not dry, when he touched it.

Writing Connection

Context clues help readers figure out the meaning of a new word. Context clues can be words or pictures. By adding pictures or definitions to your writing, you are giving your readers context clues.

Time and Order Words

Time Words

Time words show when events take place.

today	yesterday	tomorrow
last week	Thursday	next day

Take a Look

Cody wrote what he did during his spring vacation. He used time words to make it clear when he did each thing.

Last week was my spring vacation. My family drove to Lake Leland. Monday night we set up the tent by the lake. The next day we went fishing and swimming. On Wednesday it rained all day. On Thursday and Friday we went hiking in the woods. The next day we drove home.

Order Words

Using order words will make your writing clearer to your reader. **Order words** tell exactly in what order things happen.

first	later
next	last
then	finally

Take a Look

Nickoli wrote about her class field trip to the zoo. She used order words to make it clear in what order things happened.

Our trip to the zoo was fun. First we saw the monkeys and gorillas. Next we saw all kinds of bears. Then we ate lunch. Later we saw snakes and lizards. Finally we went home.

Place and Location Words

There are many words you can use to make your writing clearer to your readers. Place and location words tell where someone is or where something happens. Using these words will make your writing more specific and will help your readers understand what you write.

Here are some place and location words you might be able to use in your writing.

on	out
in	by
into	behind
near	around
above	under
over	beside
outside	inside

Take a Look

Josh wrote a paragraph about getting lost at the fair.

Getting lost at the fair is not any fun. Suddenly I turned around, and my parents weren't behind me! I walked into the rides area. I looked inside the horse barn next to the front gate. I looked everywhere. Finally I sat down to rest near the roller coaster. Then I saw my parents by the popcorn stand. I was so happy!

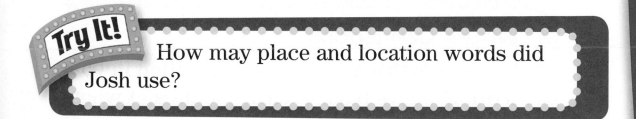

Try It!

How may place and location words did Josh use?

Position Words

Sometimes you need to show place or position in your writing.

Here are some common examples of place or position words.

above	inside	over
below	within	near
around	behind	outside
next to	on	under

FUN FACT

There are more than 30 common position or place words.

Some place words have similar meanings, such as *below*, *beneath*, and *under*.

Try It! Think of a place word that describes where you are sitting.

Writing Connection

Use words that show place or position in your writing to give readers clear pictures of what you are saying.

Compound Words

Compound words are two separate words put together to make a single word.

> day + time = daytime
> pan + cake = pancake

Sometimes you can figure out what a compound word means by looking at the words that were joined together.

> book + case = bookcase

The compound word doesn't always have the same meaning as the meanings of the two separate words.

> straw + berry = strawberry
> cart + wheel = cartwheel

Always look up words you don't know in a dictionary or glossary.

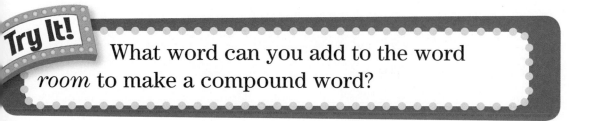

Try It! What word can you add to the word *room* to make a compound word?

Prefixes

A **prefix** is a word part that is added to the beginning of a base word to make a new word.

Here are some examples of common prefixes and their meanings.

Prefix	Prefix Meaning	Example Words
re-	again	reread, retell, refill
un-	not	unfair, unkind
over-	too much	overjoyed, overdone
mis-	bad, wrong	misspell, mistreat, misplace
pre-	before	preheat, preschool
dis-	not; opposite	disagree, dislike, disappear

Try It!

Think of other words that begin with each of the prefixes given in the chart above.

Suffixes

A **suffix** is a word part that is added to the end of a base word. Adding a suffix changes the meaning of the base word.

Here are some examples of common suffixes and their meanings.

Suffix	Suffix Meaning	Example Words
-ful	full of	joyful, hopeful, careful
-less	without	careless, painless
-est	most	deepest, saddest
-ing	acting or doing	walking, talking, running, writing
-er	one who	painter, teacher, driver
-ly	like	sadly, kindly, softly

Try It! Think of other words that end with each of the suffixes given in the above chart.

Synonyms

A word that means the same or almost the same as another word is a **synonym.** For example, *cure* and *heal* mean almost the same thing and are synonyms. Here are a few other examples of synonyms.

story—tale   couch—sofa
stop—halt   easy—simple

Try It!

Think of some synonyms for the word *nice.*

Writing Connection

Synonyms are words that mean almost the same thing. Instead of using the same words again and again, use synonyms to say things in a new way.

Antonyms

An **antonym** is a word that means the opposite of another word. Here are some common antonyms.

easy—hard	full—empty
light—dark	old—new
big—little	win—lose
true—false	hot—cold

Try It! What is an antonym for the word *happy*?

Writing Connection

Antonyms are words with opposite meanings. Use antonyms to make your writing clear and interesting to the reader.

Using the Sounds of Words

Using sounds of words in different ways can make your writing more interesting and colorful. There are many ways to use the sounds of words.

Rhyme

Words that **rhyme** have the same middle and ending sounds but different beginning sounds.

> The sun sets across the <u>land</u>,
> Flashing like diamonds on the <u>sand</u>.
>
> The butterfly dances from place to <u>place</u>,
> Giving its beauty to empty <u>space</u>.

Alliteration

Alliteration is when some of the words in a sentence or line of poetry begin with the same sound.

> Peter Piper picked a peck of pickled peppers.

Onomatopoeia

Onomatopoeia is using a word that actually makes the sound you want your readers to hear. *Bang*, *slither*, *crunch*, and *hum* are examples.

> The birds <u>swish</u> through the clear sky.
> Everyone jumped as the balloon went <u>pop</u>!

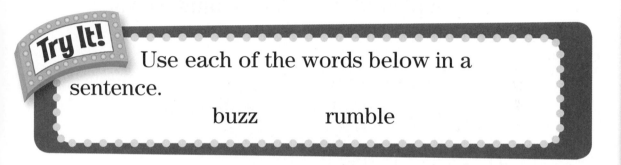

Try It! Use each of the words below in a sentence.

buzz   rumble

Repetition

When you repeat words, you can stress ideas. You can also add rhyme to your poems.

Lullaby, oh Lullaby!
Flowers are closed
And lambs are sleeping.
Lullaby, oh Lullaby!
Stars are up, the moon is peeping;
—Christina Rosetti

FUN FACT

Author Watty Piper uses repetition in the famous children's book *The Little Engine That Could.* The engine says "I think I can" over and over.

Multiple-Meaning Words

Multiple-Meaning Words are words that are spelled the same way but have different meanings. For example, the word *bank* can mean "land along a river" or "a place to keep money."

Other examples of multiple-meaning words are given below.

fair	I won a prize at the <u>fair</u>. Do you think your grade is <u>fair</u>?
bowl	Do you like to <u>bowl</u>? Put the fruit in the <u>bowl</u>.
left	My <u>left</u> shoe is missing. Only one raisin is <u>left</u> in the box.
match	Dad used a <u>match</u> to light the fire. These two gloves don't <u>match</u>.

More Multiple-Meaning Words

mean   Did Chip <u>mean</u> what he said?
             The dog has a <u>mean</u> bark.

stick   <u>Stick</u> this pin in the map.
             We stirred the paint with a <u>stick</u>.

pitcher   The juice is in the <u>pitcher</u>.
             The <u>pitcher</u> threw the ball.

can   <u>Can</u> you tie a bow?
             Open the <u>can</u> of soup, please.

Try It!   Can you think of at least two meanings
for the word *miss*?

Writing Connection

Multiple-Meaning Words are spelled the same,
but they have different meanings. Use the
correct words in your writing to say exactly
what you mean.

Homophones

Words that sound the same but have different spellings and meanings are **homophones**. For example, *blue* and *blew* sound the same, but they have different meanings and spellings. *Blue* is a color and *blew* means "did blow."

Here are some other examples of common homophones.

their/there/they're
Did you see <u>their</u> house?
We hope to see you <u>there</u>.
<u>They're</u> going to come later.

right/write
Turn <u>right</u> at the corner.
Did you <u>write</u> your report?

by/buy
I put the book <u>by</u> the door.
Tam went to <u>buy</u> some carrots.

to/two/too
I went <u>to</u> the store.
I bought <u>two</u> pencils.
I like pencils <u>too</u>.

More Homophones

through/threw
The ball went <u>through</u> the window.
Who <u>threw</u> the ball?

son/sun
Shana's <u>son</u> is my friend.
Will the <u>sun</u> come out today?

your/you're
Sign <u>your</u> name on the line.
Call me if <u>you're</u> going to be late.

Try It!

Can you think of a homophone for the word *won?* Use both words in a sentence.

Writing Connection

Homophones may sound the same, but they have different spellings and meanings. Check your writing to make sure you use the correct spelling of a homophone. Using the wrong homophone will confuse your readers!

Rules of Writing: Grammar, Usage, and Mechanics

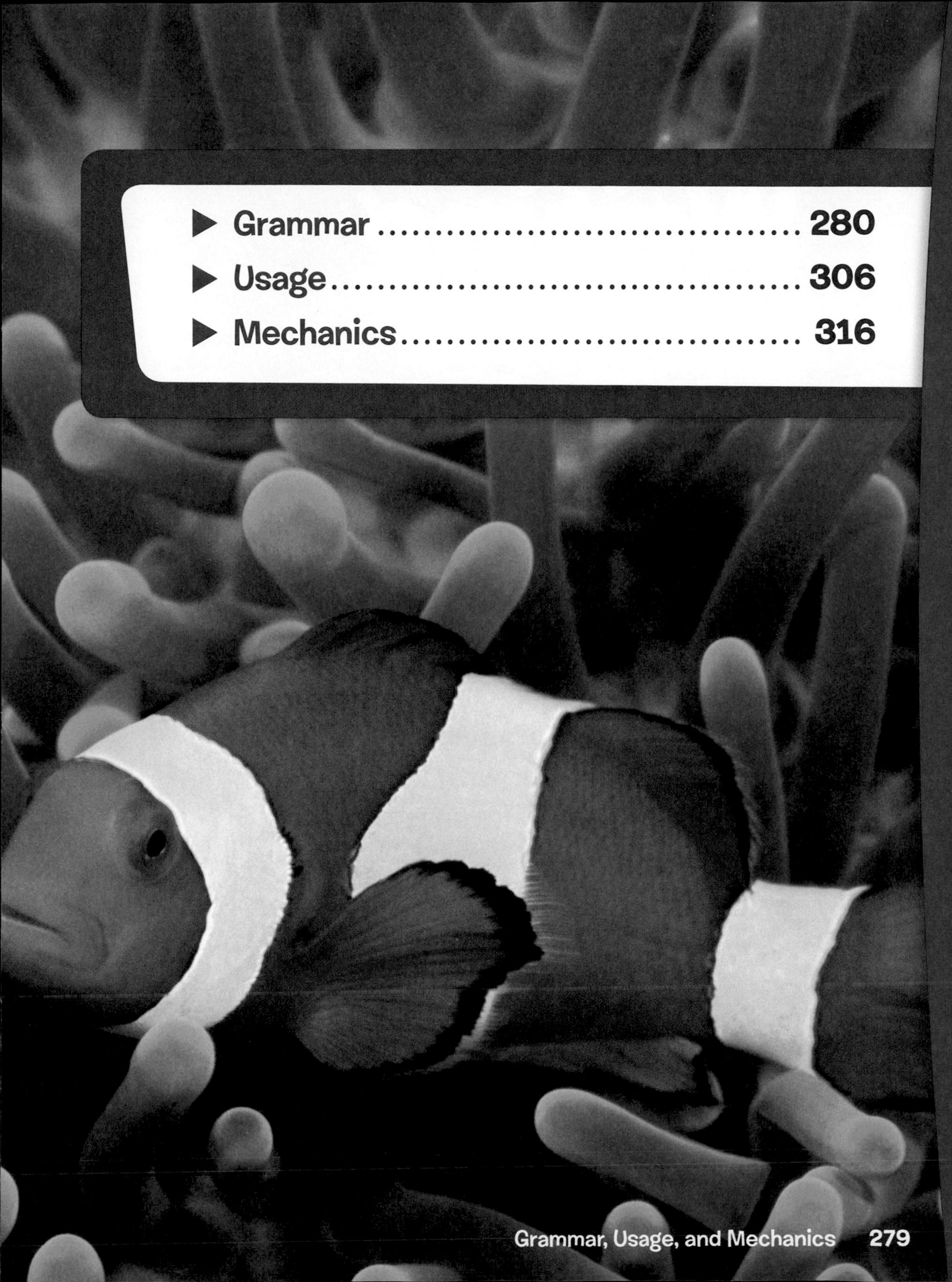

Rules of Writing

Grammar

Grammar is about how language is organized. Parts of speech, such as nouns and verbs, are grammar. The names for different parts of a sentence are grammar. Knowing about grammar helps you understand how to build sentences that make sense to your readers.

Nouns

Nouns name something. Nouns name people, places, things, and ideas. For example, think of your school, the things you carry to school, and the people you see there. The words we use for these things are all nouns.

person: woman
place: field
thing: whistle
idea: happiness

Different Kinds of Nouns

Common nouns name general things and groups of things. **Proper nouns** name particular people, places, or things. Proper nouns always begin with a capital letter.

common nouns: dog, girl, road
proper nouns: Patches, Ashley,
　　　　　　　Zigzag Road

Singular nouns name one of something.
Plural nouns name more than one.

singular:	adventure, dish, baby
plural:	adventures, dishes, babies

Some plural nouns are irregular. They are not spelled the way you might think.

singular:	wife, man, foot, child
plural:	wives, men, feet, children

Possessive nouns show ownership. Add an apostrophe-s ('s) to make singular nouns possessive. Add an apostrophe (') to make plural nouns possessive.

Possessive Nouns	
singular possessive:	Eric's bike
plural possessive:	boys' bikes

Pronouns

Pronouns take the place of nouns.

Jenna has a used **bike.**

She really likes **it.**

She and *it* are pronouns.

Pronouns						
I	me	you	he	she	it	him
her	we	us	you	they	them	

Some pronouns are singular and some are plural.

Singular Pronouns	**Plural Pronouns**
I, me	we, us
you	you
he, him	they, them
she, her	
it	

Seth went to the park.
He went to the park. (singular)

Josh called **Max and Jesse.**
Josh called **them.** (plural)

Possessive pronouns show ownership just like possessive nouns do.

> The man's home is in Alaska.
> **His** home is in Alaska.
>
> That is Sally's mitt.
> That is **her** mitt.

Possessive Pronouns					
my	mine	your	yours	his	her
hers	its	our	ours	their	theirs

Do not use an apostrophe (') with possessive pronouns.

> The bear's fur is not brown.
> **Its** fur is not brown.

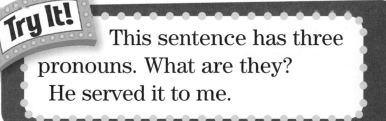

Try It! This sentence has three pronouns. What are they?
He served it to me.

Most **verbs** show action. Think of the things you do. You smile, sleep, read, and play. These words are all action verbs.

> Saltwater fish **swim** in the ocean.
> Some fish **sleep** with their eyes open.
> Some fish **eat** plants.

Linking verbs are special. They can connect parts of a sentence to make it complete. Linking verbs do not show action, but they are still verbs.

> Whales **are** mammals.
> The whale **is** large.
> That whale **was** my favorite.
> People **were** happy at the aquarium.

Here are some linking verbs.

Linking Verbs				
am	is	are	was	were

Main and Helping Verbs

The **main verb** in the sentence tells what the subject is or does.

Helping verbs are used with a main verb to tell when something is happening or has happened.

I **am** watching the Olympics.
The athletes **have** trained all year.

Here are some helping verbs.

Helping Verbs						
am	is	was	were	have	has	had

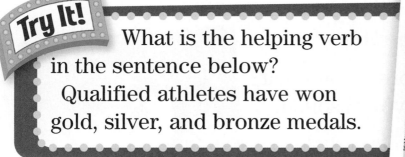

Try It! What is the helping verb in the sentence below?
Qualified athletes have won gold, silver, and bronze medals.

Adjectives

Adjectives are words that describe nouns or pronouns.

Some adjectives tell how many.

Finally, I have **two** dogs.

Some adjectives tell what kind.

They chase a **black** cat.

Articles

The words *a*, *an*, and *the* are special kinds of adjectives called **articles.**

Use *a* before a noun that begins with a consonant sound.

Emma has **a** rabbit.

Use *an* before a noun that begins with a vowel sound.

My rabbit ate **an** apple.

Use *the* with any noun.

The apple is red.

Try It!

Think of two adjectives that describe you.

Adverbs

Adverbs are words that describe verbs by telling how, where, or when.

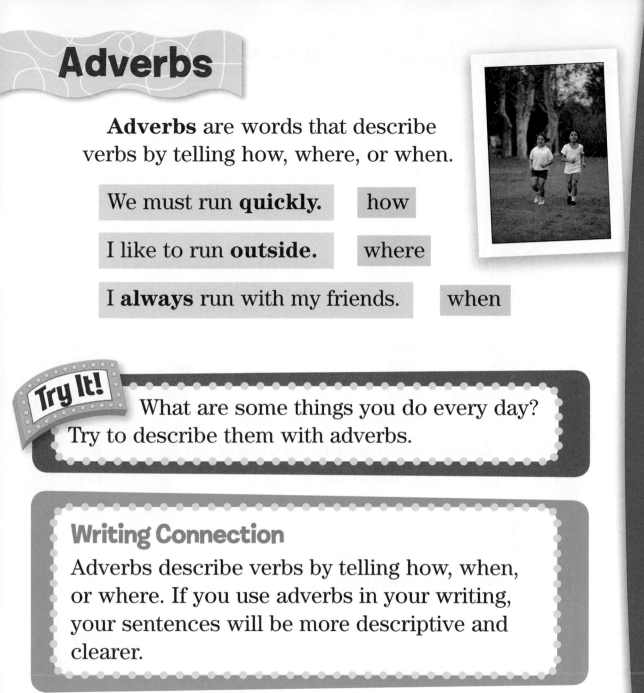

We must run **quickly.**	how
I like to run **outside.**	where
I **always** run with my friends.	when

Try It!

What are some things you do every day? Try to describe them with adverbs.

Writing Connection

Adverbs describe verbs by telling how, when, or where. If you use adverbs in your writing, your sentences will be more descriptive and clearer.

Conjunctions and Interjections

Conjunctions connect words or groups of words in a sentence.

> Diamonds **and** rubies are types of jewels.
> Diamonds can be in rings **or** necklaces.
> I like diamonds, **but** I don't like rubies.

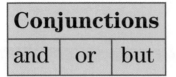

Conjunctions		
and	or	but

Interjections are words that show strong feelings. Interjections can sometimes stand alone as a sentence.

> **Oh!** Did you see that?
> **Ouch!** That hurt!

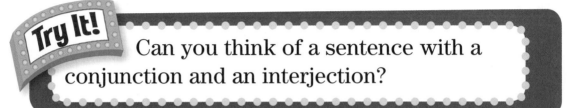

Try It! Can you think of a sentence with a conjunction and an interjection?

Sentences

A **sentence** expresses a complete thought. It begins with a capital letter and ends with a punctuation mark.

A sentence has a **subject** and a **predicate.** A **subject** tells *what* or *whom* the sentence is about. A **predicate** tells what the subject *is* or *does.*

Take a Look

Turtles crawl.

Turtles is the subject.
Crawl is the predicate.

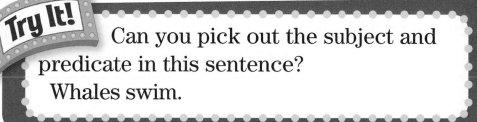

Try It!   Can you pick out the subject and predicate in this sentence?
Whales swim.

Kinds of Sentences

A **declarative** sentence makes a statement.

> The American flag has 13 stripes.

An **interrogative** sentence asks a question.

> Can we celebrate the 4th of July every day?

An **imperative** sentence gives directions or a command.

> Please wear red, white, and blue to the parade.

An **exclamatory** sentence shows strong feelings.

> I love fireworks!

Try It!

Can you change this question to a statement and use all of the same words?
Are you going to the picnic?

Writing Connection

You should try using different kinds of sentences. You can tell or ask something. You can give directions or show strong emotion.

Complete Sentences

A sentence has a subject and a predicate. A fragment is not a sentence. Something is missing. Sometimes a fragment does not have a subject. Other times it does not have a predicate.

Fragment	Ran home.
Sentence	Ally ran home.
Fragment	The little dog.
Sentence	The little dog barked a lot.

Every sentence begins with a capital letter and ends with a period or another end mark. A **run-on sentence** is two or more sentences that run together.

Run-on	Julie went camping she didn't like the bugs.
Correct	Julie went camping. She didn't like the bugs.

Compound Sentences

A **compound sentence** is made when two sentences with similar ideas are combined into one sentence. The two sentences are connected by a conjunction. The words *and, or,* and *but* are conjunctions.

Student Model

Jonathon used compound sentences to write the following paragraph about gorillas.

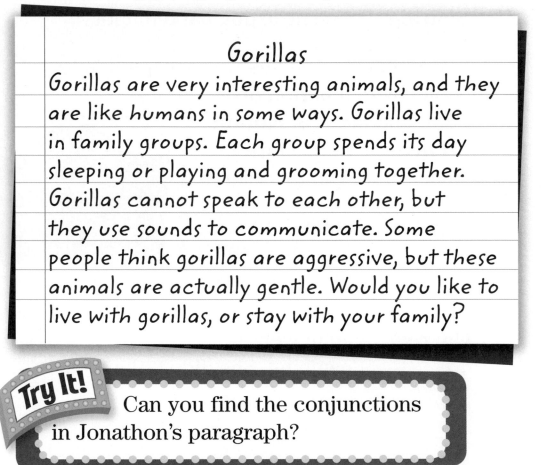

Gorillas

Gorillas are very interesting animals, and they are like humans in some ways. Gorillas live in family groups. Each group spends its day sleeping or playing and grooming together. Gorillas cannot speak to each other, but they use sounds to communicate. Some people think gorillas are aggressive, but these animals are actually gentle. Would you like to live with gorillas, or stay with your family?

Try It! Can you find the conjunctions in Jonathon's paragraph?

Parts of a Sentence

A **sentence** expresses a complete thought. A sentence has two parts: the **subject** and the **predicate.**

Subjects and Predicates

The **subject** is *what* or *whom* the sentence is about.

> **Rabbits** jump.

Rabbits is the subject.

The **predicate** tells what the subject *is* or *does.*

> The snake **slithered.**

Slithered is the predicate.

Writing Connection

There are two parts to a sentence. The subject tells who the sentence is about. The predicate tells what the subject is or does.

Sentence Problems

A **fragment** is not a sentence. Something is missing. Sometimes a subject is missing. Other times, the predicate is missing.

Fragment: Won the soccer game.
Sentence: We won the soccer game.

Fragment: My friend.
Sentence: My friend lives near the school.

Run-On Sentences

A **run-on sentence** is two or more sentences run together.

Sara studied all night she got an A on her test.

There are two ways to fix the run-on sentence.

1. Sara studied all night. She got an A on her test.
2. Sara studied all night, and she got an A on her test.

Rambling Sentences

A **rambling sentence** has too many sentences, which are usually joined by *and*.

Rambling: We went out to dinner and then we went to the movies and then we went home.

Correct: We went out to dinner and to the movies. Then we went home.

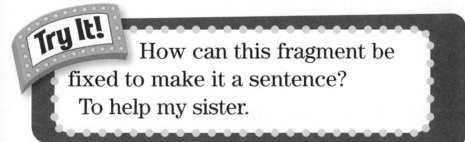

Try It! How can this fragment be fixed to make it a sentence?
To help my sister.

FUN FACT

Pencils have been used for a very long time, but pencils with erasers weren't invented until 1858.

Reading Your Writing

Fragments, run-on sentences, and rambling sentences are problems for writers and readers. Check your sentences carefully.

Paragraphs

A **paragraph** is a group of sentences that tell about the same thing.

Rules for Writing Paragraphs

▶ A paragraph begins on a new line.

▶ The first line is indented.

Topic Sentences

Many paragraphs have a **topic sentence.** It tells the main idea of a paragraph. A strong topic sentence grabs a reader's interest.

Tips for Writing Good Topic Sentences

▶ A topic sentence gives the main idea of the paragraph.

▶ Put the topic sentence at the beginning of the paragraph to let readers know what they are about to read.

Staying on the Topic

All the sentences in a paragraph should work together. Using sentences that don't fit might confuse the reader.

Take a Look

Here's a paragraph Mark wrote. He crossed out the sentence that does not stay on the topic.

There is a great new park on our block. It has swings and jungle gyms with slides. It also has sports fields. My sister and I play soccer and baseball there. There is a big pool in the middle of the park. ~~I learned to swim at the YMCA.~~ I like to swim in it with my friends. I have so much fun at the new park. I will spend all my summers there.

Types of Paragraphs

There are many reasons to write a paragraph. You can write a paragraph that

▶ tells a story

▶ explains how to do something

▶ describes something

▶ persuades someone to do something

Try It!

What type of paragraph best fits with each of the following ideas?

▶ trying to get others to recycle

▶ telling a friend about your birthday present

▶ giving directions to your local library

▶ sharing a dream you had last night

Paragraphs That Tell a Story

You can write a paragraph that tells a story. These paragraphs have a beginning, a middle, and an end.

Take a Look

Here's a paragraph that Alex wrote. It is a paragraph that tells a story.

I'll never forget my first day of school. ◀ **Beginning**
I was so scared. I didn't know anyone.
I sat in the back row of my classroom.
The kid in front of me turned around and ◀ **Middle**
asked me my name. His name is Josh. We
ate lunch together that day. We have
been friends ever since. My first day of ◀ **End**
school turned out great.

Paragraphs That Persuade

You can write a paragraph to persuade. You try to make your readers think, feel, or act a certain way. These paragraphs give reasons that support the topic.

Take a Look

Here's a paragraph that Ming wrote. This is a paragraph that persuades.

Reason 1 ▶
Reason 2 ▶
Reason 3 ▶

> Why should I have a pet turtle?
> Caring for a turtle won't cost much. I could keep my turtle in a cardboard box. Turtles eat lettuce and bugs, so it won't cost much to feed it. Turtles are quiet, so my turtle wouldn't bother my family. They don't make much of a mess. A turtle is a great pet because it's cheap, quiet, and not messy.

Paragraphs That Describe

You can write a paragraph that describes, or tells, about something. These paragraphs make a picture for the readers.

Take a Look

Here's a paragraph that Seth wrote. It is a paragraph that describes.

My tree house is great. It was built in a huge oak tree. There is a hanging ladder that I use to climb into it. It has one room with four chairs and a card table. I put posters of famous ball players on the walls. There are two windows on either side of the tree house. My tree house is a great place to hang out with friends.

Paragraphs That Explain

You can write a paragraph to give directions or tell how to do something. These paragraphs sometimes have **transition words** in them.

Transition words tell the order of things. Some examples are *first*, *next*, *then*, and *finally*.

Take a Look

Here's a paragraph that Brad wrote. This paragraph tells how to do something.

Anyone can have a lemonade stand. It's easy. First make a big pitcher of lemonade. Next set up a table in front of your house. Then put up a sign that reads, "Lemonade Sale." Finally bring your pitcher of lemonade and some paper cups to your stand. Now wait for your customers.

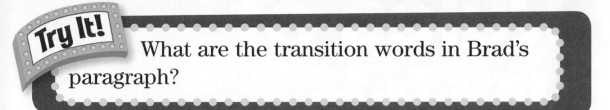

What are the transition words in Brad's paragraph?

Reading Your Writing

You write paragraphs for different reasons. You can tell a story or describe something. You can explain how to do something, or you can write to persuade.

FUN FACT

Cookbooks have paragraphs that tell how to cook food.

Rules of Writing

Usage

Usage is about how we use language when we speak and write. For example, the rules of usage tell you when to use *is* and when to use *are*. They tell you when to use *taller* and when to use *tallest*. Learning the rules of usage will help people better understand what you say and what you write.

Verb Tenses

Verbs can show that something is going on in the present.

> Jamie **sees** a deer in her neighborhood.

Verbs can show that something happened in the past.

> Jamie **saw** a deer in her neighborhood.

Verbs can be changed from the present to the past. You can do this by adding *-ed* to the end of some verbs.

> I talk.
>
> I talk**ed.**

Some verbs do not add *-ed* to change from the present to the past. They change in other ways.

> **Present** I sing.
>
> **Past** I sang.

Using the correct tense of a verb is important in writing. A **future-tense verb** tells about something that *will* happen in the future.

Present-tense verbs can be changed to future-tense verbs by adding the word *will*.

Present Tense	Future Tense
sing	will sing
talk	will talk

Past-tense verbs can be changed to future-tense verbs by adding the word *will*. However, the verb also will need to be changed.

Past Tense	Future Tense
washed	will wash
grew	will grow

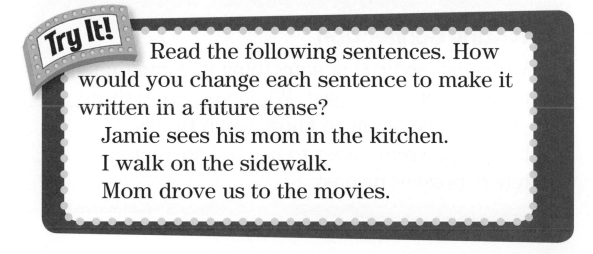

Try It!

Read the following sentences. How would you change each sentence to make it written in a future tense?

Jamie sees his mom in the kitchen.

I walk on the sidewalk.

Mom drove us to the movies.

Linking Verbs in Present and Past

Linking verbs can also show present and past.

Present	
Singular verb	The bird **is** small.
Plural verb	The birds **are** small.
Past	
Singular verb	The bird **was** here.
Plural verb	The birds **were** here.

Try It!

Look back at the sentences about Jamie on page 306. How did that verb change from present to past?

Writing Connection

Verbs can show that something is going on in the present or the past. When you are writing, your readers want to know when things happen, so remember to use the correct verb tense, present or past.

Subject/Verb Agreement

A subject and verb must agree in a sentence. That means the correct form of a verb must go with the subject. **Singular** means "one." **Plural** means "more than one."

If the subject is singular, the verb must agree with it.

> A plant grows.
> The leaf withers.

If the subject is plural, the verb must agree with a plural subject.

> The plants grow.
> The leaves wither.

Making Verbs Agree

Look at the sentences below. What do you notice about verbs with singular subjects?

These verbs end with an *s*.

> The plant needs water.
> The leaf dies.

The verbs that go with plural subjects do not end with an *s*.

> The plants need water.
> The leaves die.

Singular and Plural Subjects and Linking Verbs

Here are the rules for using linking verbs.

▶ Use *is* with singular subjects.
The star **is** far away.

▶ Use *are* with plural subjects.
The stars **are** far away.

▶ Use *has* with singular subjects.
The planet **has** many colors.

▶ Use *have* with plural subjects and the pronoun *I*.
The planets **have** many colors.
I **have** many pictures of the planets.

Try It!

Which sentence has a singular subject? Which sentence has a plural subject? Do the verbs agree with their subjects in both sentences?

The sky has many stars.
Those stars are yellow.

Comparing with Adjectives

An **adjective** describes nouns or pronouns. You can use adjectives to compare.

Most adjectives that compare two nouns or pronouns end in *-er*.

A tree is **taller** than a bush.

Most adjectives that compare more than two nouns or pronouns end in *-est*.

The pine tree is the **tallest** tree in the yard.

Some adjectives don't add *-er* or *-est* to compare. Instead, they use *more* and *most*. Use *more* to compare two things. Use *most* to compare more than two things.

A parrot is **more** beautiful than a robin.

The parrot is the **most** beautiful bird of all.

Try It! Make a sentence that compares the seals to whales.

Contractions

A **contraction** puts two words together. Some letters are taken out. An apostrophe (') takes the place of the letters that are taken out.

Here are some common contractions that you use every day as you talk. This is what they look like when they are written.

Common Contractions	
I am ⟶ I'm	she is ⟶ she's
I have ⟶ I've	is not ⟶ isn't
I will ⟶ I'll	did not ⟶ didn't
We are ⟶ we're	should not ⟶ shouldn't

Try It! Look at each pair of sentences. Find the contractions. What letters were taken out?

I will fix the mistake.

I'll fix the mistake.

You did not have to do that.

You didn't have to do that.

Word Order in Sentences

The words in a sentence must come in the correct order. If the words are not in the correct order, the sentence will not make sense. Every complete sentence has a subject and a predicate. Usually, the subject of the sentence comes first.

Take a Look

Correct Word Order	Lilly is playing with Mary.
Incorrect Word Order	Mary with Lilly is playing.
Correct Word Order	My birthday party is on Saturday.
Incorrect Word Order	Saturday is my birthday party.

Try It! Can you put the following words in the correct order to make a sentence? Barked and wagged his tail the dog.

Rules of Writing

Mechanics

The rules of mechanics are very important in writing. How and when to use punctuation marks is part of mechanics. When to use capital letters is part of mechanics. Writers who know and follow these rules make it much easier for readers to understand what they write.

End Marks and Abbreviations

Every sentence must end with a period, a question mark, or an exclamation point. These are all **punctuation marks.**

End a sentence with a period (.) when it tells something.

> Hawaii is made of islands.

End a sentence with a question mark (?) when it asks something.

> Have you been to the island of Maui?

End a sentence with an exclamation point (!) when it shows strong feeling.

> It's such an exciting place!

Other Uses for Periods

▶ Use a period after an abbreviation. An abbreviation is a shortened form of a word.

> **Mr.** Robert Payne   Curly **Rd.**

▶ Use a period after initials.

> **E. B.** White   Mary **A.** Taylor

Commas

A **comma** (,) is another punctuation mark. Commas are most often used to separate things in a sentence.

▶ Use commas in dates between the day and the year.
    January 31, 2003

▶ Put commas after the greeting and closing in a friendly letter.
    Dear Jenny,
    Love,
    Patty

▶ Use a comma between a city and state in an address.
    Salt Lake City, Utah

▶ In a list of three or more things, put a comma after each word that comes before *and* or *or.*
    Elm, oak, and maple are all trees.
    I don't like spinach, okra, or squash.

▶ In a sentence with someone's exact words, use a comma to separate the quotation from the person who said it.
    Donna said, "I like dinosaurs!"

Quotation Marks and Underlining

Quotation marks are another type of punctuation. They are used in many ways.

Use quotation marks before and after a speaker's exact words.

> Zack said, "I will play my tuba in the gymnasium."

Use quotation marks for titles of stories, songs, and poems.

> Sue just read the story "The Kite in Flight."

Underlining is a way to identify titles of books, plays, and magazines.

> Have you read <u>Ryan's Red Room</u>?

Writing Connection

Quotation marks and underlining provide special information to readers. Quotation marks signal when someone is speaking. Underlining signals some type of published writing.

Apostrophes and Colons

Apostrophes (') are another type of punctuation mark.

> ▶ Apostrophes are used to make a contraction.
> I will wash my bike.
> I'll wash my bike.
> ▶ Apostrophes are also used to show ownership.
> Rosa's bike is blue.

Another type of punctuation is the **colon** (:). Here are some ways that you can use the colon.

> ▶ Colons are used to introduce a list.
> I need these things from the supermarket: milk, eggs, and bread.
> ▶ Colons also separate the hour and the minutes when you write the time.
> Will you pick me up at 7:30 p.m?

Writing Connection

Apostrophes are used to make a contraction or to show ownership. Colons are used to introduce a list or when you write the time. Remember to put these punctuation marks where you need them.

Capital Letters

Capital letters are an important part of writing. We use capital letters every time we write sentences. Here are some suggestions to help you use them.

▶ The first word in a sentence always begins with a capital letter.

My brother likes scrambled eggs.

▶ The word *I* is always a capital letter.

My dad and **I** will be there.

▶ Names of proper nouns begin with capital letters.

Rose **H**arris   **G**ill **L**ake

▶ People's titles and initials begin with capital letters.

Dr. Ruby **G**oode   **J. A. C**ooper

▶ Words used as names begin with capital letters.

Mom **D**ad **G**randma **G**randpa

▶ Days, months, and holidays begin with capital letters.

Thursday **N**ovember **T**hanksgiving

More Places to Use Capital Letters

▶ Cities, states, and countries begin with capital letters.

    Chicago   **I**llinois   **U**nited **S**tates

▶ Titles of books, newspapers, stories, songs, and poems begin with capital letters.

    We sang "**H**appy **B**irthday" to Josh.

    Have you read the book *The Seven Sisters*?

▶ The first word a speaker says begins with a capital letter even if it's not the first word in the sentence.

    Emily said, "**M**y brother will be home soon."

▶ The greeting and closing of letters begin with a capital letter.

    Dear Sammy,   **Y**our friend,
                           Eddie

Writing Connection

There are many reasons to use capital letters. Remember to check for them in your writing.

Glossary

A

adjective   a word that describes a noun or pronoun

adverb   a word that describes a verb by telling how, when, or where

antonym   a word that means the opposite, or almost the opposite, of another word

apostrophe (')   a punctuation mark used with possessive nouns to show ownership and with contractions to show where letters have been left out

audience   the person or people who read what you write

C

characters   the people or animals in a story

colon (:)   a punctuation mark used to introduce a list in a sentence. It is also used to separate the hour and the minutes when writing the time.

comma (,)   a punctuation mark used to separate items in a series, in dates, and in cities and states

compound word   two or more words put together to make a new word, such as *daytime*

conferencing   a meeting in which a writer and teacher or other classmate discuss the writing and make suggestions to make it better

conjunction   a word that connects other words or ideas. The words *and, or,* and *but* are conjunctions.

D

declarative sentence   a sentence that makes a statement and ends with a period

dialogue   the talk or conversation between two or more characters in a story or play

drafting   the part of the writing process in which you write a draft, or first try, of what you want to say

E

editing/proofreading   the part of the writing process during which you read your writing to check for mistakes in grammar, spelling, punctuation, and capitalization

exclamation point (!)   a punctuation mark used at the end of an exclamatory sentence or after an interjection

exclamatory sentence   a sentence that shows strong feeling and ends with an exclamation point

F

fairy tale   a story that has make-believe characters and places. A fairy tale usually has a happy ending.

fiction   a made-up story that entertains readers

fragment   a group of words that is not a complete thought

free-verse poem   a type of poem that does not rhyme or have a pattern

friendly letter   a letter you write to a friend or relative

G

get-well note   a special note or card you send to someone when he or she is sick

H

homographs   words that are spelled the same way but have different meanings

homophones   words that sound the same but have different spellings and meanings

I

imperative sentence   a sentence that gives a command or makes a request. It can end with a period or an exclamation point.

interjection   a word that shows strong feeling. It can sometimes stand alone as a sentence.

interrogative sentence   a sentence that asks a question and ends with a question mark

invitation   a note or card you send to invite someone to a party

J

journal   a place where you can write about your thoughts and ideas

M

metaphor   a comparison of two unlike things without using *like* or *as:* The grass was a soft, green carpet.

multiple-meaning words   words that are spelled the same but have different meanings

N

nonfiction   based on facts. It contains facts about real things, people, and events.

noun   a word that names a person, place, or thing

O

onomatopoeia   using a word that imitates the sound it describes, such as *swish* and *pop*

order words   words that tell in what order things happen, such as *first, next,* and *last*

organization   the way writing is put together, including a good opening, correct order, and an interesting ending

P

paragraph   a group of sentences about one idea

period (.)   a type of punctuation mark found at the end of statements and after abbreviations and initials

personal narrative   a form of writing in which the writer tells something that has really happened in his or her own life

personification   describing nonhuman things as if they were human. The old car *coughed* and *sputtered.*

persuade   to try to get someone to think in a certain way or do a certain thing

picture book   a book in which the pictures are as important as the words in telling the story

play   a true or make-believe story that is acted out for an audience

plot   the action or events in a story. Often, the plot tells about a problem and how it is solved.

plural   more than one

poetry   a type of writing that joins the sound and meaning of words to create ideas and feelings

portfolio   a place to keep your finished and unfinished writing. You can also keep writing ideas and word lists in your portfolio.

position words   words that show place or location, such as *under* and *over*

poster   a big sign used to share information with others

prefix   a word part that is added to the beginning of a base word to make a new word

presentation   the way your writing looks when you are ready to publish

prewriting   a part of the writing process. During prewriting, you choose a topic, gather ideas, and make a plan.

pronoun   a word that takes the place of a noun

proofreading marks   marks that are used when proofreading someone's writing

publishing   the part of the writing process in which you share your writing

purpose   your reason for writing. The purpose could be to entertain, to inform, or to persuade.

Q

question mark (?)   a punctuation mark used at the end of sentences that ask questions

quotation marks (" ")   punctuation marks used to show the exact words a speaker says. They are also used for titles of stories and poems.

R

realistic story   a made-up story that did not happen, but the characters, places, and events in the story seem real

report   a piece of writing that gives information about a specific topic

revising   a part of the writing process in which you make changes to improve what you have written

rhyme   repeating syllables that sound alike, such as at the ends of lines of poetry

S

sentence   a group of words that expresses a complete thought

setting   the time and place of a story

simile   compares two unlike things using the words *like* or *as*. The snow was like a white blanket on the ground.

singular   one

suffix   a word part that is added to the end of a base word to make a new word

summary   writing that tells the main idea and main points of a longer piece of writing

synonym   a word that means the same, or almost the same, as another word

T

thank-you note   a note or card you send to someone to thank them for a gift or for doing something special for you

time line   a graphic organizer that shows events that have happened in the correct order

time words   words that show when events take place, such as *today*, *tomorrow*, and *yesterday*

topic   a subject one chooses to write about

topic sentence   a sentence that tells the main idea of a paragraph. Topic sentences most often occur in expository or persuasive writing.

V

verb   a word that shows action or state of being

W

writing process   a plan to follow when writing. The steps are prewriting, drafting, revising, editing/proofreading, and publishing.

Index

The **index** is a list of words and the page numbers on which they appear. It lists the different topics that are included in this Handbook. The entries are listed in alphabetical order. Look in the list for the word you want to find, and then look at the page number where it can be found. The index is a good tool. Learn to use it because it can save you a lot of time.

▶ **Photo Credits:**